# AN **A**MERICAN NURSE
# **A**MIDST CHAOS

Dear Marie,

I hope you enjoy the book. You inspired me in the annual magnet conference

Gladys morris

16 NOV 2004

# AN **A**MERICAN NURSE
**A**MIDST CHAOS

## GLADYS MOURO

AMERICAN UNIVERSITY OF BEIRUT PRESS

SECOND EDITION

© 2001 American University of Beirut Press

Published by American University of Beirut Press
American University of Beirut
Beirut, Lebanon

First printing 1999
2000

Printed in Beirut, Lebanon
ISBN 9953-9011-0-4

# Contents

# Dedication

This book is dedicated to the American University of Beirut, the institution I have grown to love and consider my home; to those friends who supported me in my decision to remain at AUB; to my family, who experienced pain because of my decision; to the nursing profession and my loyal nursing colleagues who may not recognize the measure of their importance in society; to those friends who died because of the terrible war or lost a loved one or went into depression; and most of all, to Dr. Samuel P. Asper who made this book come true.

The AUB Medical Center

# Preface

Why did I write this book? The idea never occurred to me until one day in 1982 when Dr. Samuel Asper, who was one of the few people who encouraged me to remain in Lebanon during the war, urged me to keep a diary of my experiences. Dr. Asper had been Dean of the Medical School at the American University of Beirut from 1973 to 1978 and, since then, he and his wife, Ann, have remained two of my most supportive and loving friends. There was also my brother George, who envied his adventurous sister and kept telling me, "You should write a book, Gladys. I wish I had the chance to do what you are doing."

It was not easy living through the war and even more difficult to record my experiences on a daily basis and then write a book. I am a nurse, not a writer. But once I began, I became more and more convinced of the value of putting it all down on paper—to show the world what tough times the doctors, nurses and administrative staff of a hospital in war-torn Lebanon lived through, day after day for fifteen years. For all of us, it was a unique experience that taught us so much about giving, survival, patience

Medical gatehouse
circa 1893

and responsibility; about learning how to handle stress, sorrow and loneliness; and how to sustain hope, express love, control frustration and suppress anger despite it all.

I hope this book will remind all nurses that helping people is in itself a reward. I especially hope it will tell those who were burnt out in the process, who gave beyond their capacities to endure, how important and valuable their efforts were. Perhaps what I have written will also tell all those responsible for the management of a hospital that wise decision-making and proper delegation of authority—plus flexibility to handle the unexpected—are more essential than ever during crisis and that the capabilities of those in such positions are vital to the smooth functioning and survival of an institution. I also want to set the record straight for the many people who look upon the Lebanese as no more than a bunch of thugs fighting turf battles.

Determination, faith and dedication—plus a measure of courage I never knew I had—saw me through the misery of Lebanon's war. I learned how to survive in the most difficult of situations, to assume the most challenging responsibilities and to develop as a leader. I believe that many faced with similar problems can do the same; I believe that dedication to their profession, to their values and to their country can, with perseverance, move mountains.

Many people, friends, family and strangers alike, wondered why I stayed on at AUB. I myself often had doubts. But the more people begged me to leave, the more I wanted to stay. The primary driving force was that I felt needed. And then there was the challenge of it all, the not giving up in spite of the risks. There were times when I feared being kidnapped, when I was unable to circulate outside the hospital or express my feelings, when I suffered terrible nightmares. In a way, I was kidnapped—not locked in a cell, but emotionally held as a hostage of fear.

Abandoning AUB would have been like abandoning a child. Moreover, it was an American institution and being an American added to my sense of loyalty. I felt I had an obligation to America to keep this institution alive and running. I also felt an equally strong obligation not only to my profession but also to Lebanon, the land of my mother's birth, and to its people, for whom I have great affection.

Now I am forty, alone, without a husband or children. Instead of enjoying the normal pleasures of life, I find I have spent the years of my youth on just trying to survive and helping others to survive. Was it worth it? Should I have married? Should I have returned to the US to continue with post-graduate studies and further develop my potential? Should I have gone to the Gulf, like so many others, and made lots of money? I have no answer to these questions. I only know that I had a strong compulsion to stay in Lebanon, that somehow my staying would make a difference to the hospital, to the University and to Lebanon.

*Gladys Mouro*
*Assistant Hospital Director*
*American University of Beirut Medical Center*
*Beirut, Lebanon*
*1998*

# Acknowledgments

This book was written after Dr. Samuel Asper encouraged me in his letters from the USA to do so. I couldn't get myself to put in writing what we went through. Had it not been for Dr. Asper's persistence, this book would never have been completed.

I would like to express my appreciation to the following people for their support and counsel. Generous support for the preparation and publication of this book in all its phases has been provided by the AUB Fund Foundation. The late Dr. Alfred Howell chairman of the foundation, believed in and encouraged this project; he never gave up with Dr. Asper. Thanks to Dr. Calvin Plimpton, who followed up after Dr. Howell's death, and the AUB administration both in Beirut and New York for their continuous support. To Dr. Fredric P. Herter, who never lost confidence in me, to Eileen O'Connor who was beside me during my grief when I had to leave for the U.S. for a period of time. To Dr. Thomas Morris, who had faith in my potentials and encouraged me to go on supporting AUB.

Special acknowledgements go to Mr. George Tomey

and Dr. Adnan Mroueh, who in 1989 helped me return to continue my mission at AUB.

Special thanks also go to Dr. Makhlouf Haddadin in seeing this project through, to Dr. Abdul Hamid Hallab, whose support I needed when I was forced to go to the Gulf. I would also like to thank Dr. Raif Nassif for the review of the first draft and his useful comments along with Dr. Asper's, and for strongly recommending the manuscript for publication. I tried to incorporate almost all of their suggestions.

I am extremely grateful to Helen Khal, the editor, for an outstanding job and to Anissa Rafeh, the copy editor at the AUB's Publications Office for a superb job in a short time.

To my colleagues in nursing, my assistant Chantal Madi, Supervisors, nurse Managers, secretaries, and nursing Staff I thank them for supporting me for the past twenty-one years and to my ex-secretary, Nora, who typed the manuscript.

Finally, I cannot forget the special friends who were around to support me and never gave up on me in spite of my stubbornness to remain. I owe them a great deal.

To my family, my mother, brothers George and André, I am sorry to have chosen to remain in Lebanon and deprive you of me all these years. I am grateful for your support and belief in me.

# "This Extraordinary Person"

I first met Gladys Mouro at the University of Pennsylvania in 1981, where her good friend, Dr. Samuel P. Asper, was Deputy Director of the American College of Physicians. He and I had met several times and he told me about Gladys and his concern for her professional development. She was clearly a rising star in the nursing structure at the hospital of the American University of Beirut, but believed she needed to advance her education in order to improve her performance and move forward.

It took no more than ten minutes to realize that Penn's School of Nursing would benefit from having this extraordinary person a student and alumna. My colleague, Dr. Anne Keane, the Director of the Graduate Program in Adult Health and Illness, was equally impressed and agreed.

Gladys entered the program in the fall of 1982 and was a fine student. She brought her intelligence, sensitivity and commitment to the program and enhanced the experiences of all who came in contact with her. Her performance was exemplary and we would have liked her to remain at Penn and complete her Ph.D. She, however, was convinced that she needed to return "home" to Lebanon to continue her work there and to provide leadership and support to her nursing colleagues.

The situation in Beirut worsened after her return, and her Penn friends had great concern for her emotional and physical safety. Her letters assured us that despite the problems in the country and in the hospital itself, she was well and achieving her mission in life. Her letters brought us joy, but did not really eliminate our concerns.

Gladys Mouro is a woman who could have done anything she chose. She has the personality, skills and intelligence to place her in the forefront of any profession and the educational background to place her in leadership roles in nursing. She has chosen to devote her life so far to her triple loyalties—America, Lebanon and nursing. Her achievements are so noteworthy that one would think that the person with these accomplishments would be at the twilight of a career. I know that we can expect to see a great deal more from Gladys Mouro; and I, for one, will be happy to see what comes next.

*Claire M. Fagin, Ph.D., R.N., Dean Emeritus*
*The Leadership Professor*
*University of Pennsylvania, School of Nursing*
*Philadelphia*
*June 1995*

# Prologue

In this country known as Lebanon, on the eastern shores of the Mediterranean Sea, there is a small island of inestimable value called the American University of Beirut. This University includes a medical center that has graduated many professionals now prominent in the world medical community. It also treated the largest number of casualties throughout the fifteen years of war in Lebanon. Before telling you about my experiences during those terrible years, I want to relate the story of AUB itself. Its history represents a 134-year saga of noble purpose that shaped the University's unique character and forged the remarkable strength it needed to survive those years.

In 1862, the American Board of Commissioners for Foreign Missions asked the American missionary in Lebanon, Dr. Daniel Bliss, to withdraw from his evangelical work in Lebanon and found a college of higher education that would include a medical school. It was felt that this college, which would be based on American educational standards, should be administered independently from the mission and be maintained by its own funds. In

An aerial view of the American University of Beirut campus

August of that year, Dr. Bliss sailed with his family for the United States to solicit funds for the new enterprise. By August 1864, he had raised $100,000, but because of inflation during the American Civil War, it was decided that he should leave the dollar fund in the U.S. to appreciate in value and raise a sterling fund in England to use in establishing the college. After collecting the pound equivalent of $4,000 in England, Dr. Bliss returned to Lebanon in March 1866.

While the money was being raised, the State of New York on April 24, 1863, granted a charter for the new school under the name of the Syrian Protestant College (at that time, Lebanon and Syria were one entity under Ottoman control). The college opened in Beirut on December 3, 1866, with its first class of sixteen students.

The Honorable William Dodge, Sr., then Treasurer of the Board of Trustees, laid the cornerstone of College Hall, the first building to be constructed on the University's present campus in Ras Beirut, on December 7, 1871. At the ceremony, President Daniel Bliss expressed the guiding principles of the college in these words:

> *This college is for all conditions and classes of men,*
> *without regard to color, nationality, race or religion.*
> *A man, white, black or yellow, Christian, Jew,*
> *Mohammedan or heathen, may enter and enjoy all*
> *the advantages of the institution for three, four or eight*
> *years, and go out believing in one God, in many Gods,*
> *or in no God. But it will be impossible for anyone to*
> *continue with us long without knowing what we*
> *believe to be the truth and our reasons for that belief.*

The language of the people was Arabic and it seemed only natural to the missionaries that they teach in Arabic.

Sixteen years later, in 1882, English became the language of instruction. All the missionaries spoke, read and wrote Arabic. Dr. Cornelius Van Dyck, one of the first professors appointed to the Medical Department, had contributed to a magnificent translation of the Bible into Arabic, published in 1884.

The Medical Department opened in 1867. A preparatory school was established in 1871, as was a Department of Pharmacy (which closed in 1979). By 1873, College Hall and the first medical building had been completed and were in use. The bell in the clock tower of College Hall was installed and struck the hour for the first time on March 14, 1874.

Through the decades, as one discipline after another was added, the college grew into a full-fledged University. A Department of Commerce, later incorporated into the School of Arts and Sciences, opened in 1900. A nurses' training facility, one of the first in the Middle East, admitted its first five students in 1905 (it now offers a four-year program leading to a BS in nursing). A School of Dentistry opened in 1910 and continued to operate until its closure in 1940. In 1951, the Faculty of Engineering and Architecture was established; in 1952 came the Faculty of Agriculture; and in 1954, the School of Public Health (now the Faculty of Health Sciences) opened.

On November 18, 1920, the Board of Regents of the State of New York changed the name of the institution from the Syrian Protestant College to the American University of Beirut. Dr. Daniel Bliss retired as president in 1902 and since then AUB has had ten other presidents. By the end of August 1998, the total number of degrees, diplomas, and certificates awarded since June 1870 had reached 60,764. One third of all AUB's graduates are women.

The University campus is situated in the western sector of

Beirut, with a commanding view of the Mediterranean Sea and the soaring snow-capped mountains of Lebanon to the east. Located on its seventy acres are administrative and classroom buildings, two halls for student activities, two men's and four women's dormitories, faculty apartments and athletic fields.

Adjoining the campus is the Medical Center, an integral part of AUB's history, whose modest beginnings and subsequent growth would make a story in itself. As a private teaching institution, it serves Lebanon in the training of medical, nursing and paramedical professionals. As a hospital, it offers comprehensive health care services and extensive tertiary resources through its specialized care units. Initially known as the Medical Department when it was established in 1867, one year after the Syrian Protestant College was founded, it evolved from a few rooms in a rented building to the modern multi-million-dollar facility it is today.

During the first decades of this century, the College saw the need to add new clinical specialties to its medical program of patient care and teaching. Gradually, as it acquired the land required to expand, its mini-medical center began to grow in earnest. In 1905, three pavilions to treat diseases of women and children opened. Laboratory buildings, student and nurses' dormitories, dietary and laundry facilities followed. In 1930, the Outpatient Clinic was established and, in 1953, a pediatric wing was added.

After World War II, however, it had become apparent that the existing hospital facilities could no longer cope with the demands of modern medicine. Expansion was viewed as mandatory and it was decided that instead of adding to existing facilities, what was needed was a large, totally new hospital. Intensive planning, combined with concentrated effort on funding, began in 1959. On May 8, 1963, ground was broken for the first phase of construction.

On June 26, 1970, the new American University of Beirut Medical Center officially opened its doors. The hospital, organized under a director who reports to the Dean of the Faculty of Medicine, is composed of eleven clinical departments and twenty-nine allied service departments. The active medical staff consists of more than 194 full and part-time physicians who also assume teaching responsibilities and undertake ongoing clinical research projects. The Center's Clinical Pathology Department is the most extensive in Lebanon and functions as a reference laboratory for several area hospitals. A Physical Medicine Program dealing with prosthetics-orthotics also provides specialized services for the evaluation and treatment of physically disabled patients—services that were much in need during and after the war. An ambulatory unit, staffed by attending and resident physicians, treats more than 50,000 patients a year and provides services of all kinds.

The Medical Center has been accredited by the U.S. Joint Commission on Accreditation of Hospitals.

## Chapter One
# Before the War

I was born in the United States, in the small town of Pawtucket in the small state of Rhode Island, where I lived, safe and secure, with my mother and father and my two older brothers, George and André. I had heard about Lebanon from my mother, who is originally Lebanese from Zahlé. One summer, she took me with her on a trip there to visit her father. Lebanon, thousands of miles away, it was like travelling to another planet. I was only a child then and had never been that far away from home. The memory of that visit, the excitement of it all, remained vivid all through the years.

In 1973, when I was a freshman at the University of New Hampshire and planning to enter its School of Nursing, I decided to go to Lebanon instead to pursue my Bachelor of Science degree in nursing at the American University of Beirut. I intended to return to the U.S. after graduation. Little did I know I would stay in Lebanon for decades and watch the tragedy of this beautiful land unfold.

My only goal in life had always been to become a nurse.

AUB medical gate

7

I remember how I used to play "nurse" as a child, how I would wrap my mother's leg in a towel and take her temperature. And I thought living in Lebanon would be an exciting adventure—which turned out to be the understatement of the century! My family did not like the idea of my going so far away, but who listens to family at the age of eighteen? My father had died and I was living with my brother George, who had appointed himself my surrogate parent. His position, of course, was negative; but against his wishes, I applied to the AUB School of Nursing, was accepted as a sophomore student, and proceeded to pack my bags.

I was, after all, going to a country I had fallen in love with as a child. I was going to study at a university well known for its academic standards, and nursing was all I ever wanted to do with my life. Now, finally,

Building 56

shy and timid Gladys Mouro would be travelling halfway across the world to enter the real world of doctors, nurses and hospitals in a country that would eventually become her adopted home.

I arrived in Lebanon in the fall of 1974 and happily settled into my new life—mingling and making friends with the many students of different nationalities at AUB; travelling around a country that was smaller than Rhode Island in size, but so imposing in geography; snow-skiing on high mountain slopes in the morning and water-skiing alongside sandy seashores in the afternoon. It was all so fascinating and beautiful—a bountiful land of succulent fruits and vegetables; a dramatic landscape of soaring mountains, sheltered valleys and fertile plains, with umbrella pine forests and the majestic biblical Cedars of Lebanon; and with a stimulating and pleasurable social and cultural life that combined East and West, old and new. I fell in love with Lebanon all over again.

In the spring of 1975, my brother George visited me to find out first-hand how I was faring and why I insisted on staying in Lebanon. He came with his wife Cynthia and I took time off to show them around. We went to the Cedars, to Baalbeck, to the castles of Byblos and Sidon, to the caves of Jeita, and to the Casino of Lebanon—a fabulous entertainment complex, complete with gambling rooms, night club and extravaganza shows featuring beautiful women in glittering costumes that rivaled anything to be seen in Las Vegas or Paris.

I was so happy to show them Lebanon and so proud to introduce George and Cynthia to my friends. George was a lieutenant in the U.S. Army at the time and looked very impressive in his uniform (today he is a colonel in the Reserves). When he saw how committed I was to continuing my education in Lebanon and how attached I had become to the country and especially to the University, he agreed that I could stay, but on one condition: that I return to the U.S. as soon as I graduated. Little did we know that the country was literally on the brink of war.

At AUB, I had been assigned to a women's dormitory called Building 56 simply because it was the fifty-sixth building on campus, although it was officially named the Bayard Dodge, Jr. Building when it was built in 1954. It was conveniently connected to the hospital by an underground tunnel, allowing us to go back and forth without going outside (later it would serve as a welcome shelter during bombardments).

In my junior year, I was appointed resident counselor of Building 56, a position that required me to assist the head resident in her duties. The job helped develop my administrative capabilities and prepared me to shoulder all the demanding responsibilities I was soon to face in Lebanon's war. It was as though fate had decreed this assignment specifically to increase my attachment and commitment to AUB and Lebanon and, at the same time, provide me with the multi-leveled skills I would need to cope with the long and difficult years ahead. I was proud to be wearing the apricot uniform of the AUB nursing student, but I could hardly wait for the day of graduation when my uniform would change to glorious white.

I loved every minute of my student days. Rotating through the clinical units, totally absorbed and fascinated by everything around me—the busy, focused activities of doctors and nurses in white moving up and down the halls; the patients, young and old, warmly greeting their many visitors. I enjoyed looking after the patients, talking to them and to their visitors, and being so directly involved in the round-the-clock activities of a hospital. And in this culture so different from mine, the challenge of communicating with the Lebanese kept me constantly on my toes. It was then that I realized I needed to learn how to speak Arabic.

## Chapter Two
# The Civil War Begins

The spark of what proved to be the ugliest, longest and most devastating war ever fought in this region was struck in April 1975. Over the next fifteen years, more than 150,000 people would be killed and many times more wounded, adding up to more than one-third of the population. For those who lived through this nightmare, it was a deadly game of run, hide and survive. As I look back over those years, I wonder how we made it. To this date, although the fighting has ceased, disturbing under-currents of the war's political, social and psychological damage persist.

Along with all the human loss, misery and destruction it caused, the conflict disrupted the day-to-day activities of all. The city itself became a battlefield and suddenly most of the amenities of normal life disappeared. Water, fuel and electricity services were cut, telephone service became erratic, fresh food supplies became scarce, and we seldom knew a peaceful night's sleep. Slowly, as the fabric of this once vibrant society disintegrated, we saw the

Traffic jam in Beirut: trying to escape the mayhem

beauty of Lebanon die and I soon became involved in horrors that made me wish at times that I, too, would die. But I learned how to survive, how to improvise and cope, how never to give up despite impossible odds. I became strong and persistent because I believed in what I was doing. It was a take-it-or-leave-it situation and I definitely did not want to leave. I was needed and I wanted to prove to myself that I could make a difference.

Beirut, at the time, had about one million inhabitants, and the fighting that broke out between the eastern and western sectors divided the city in half at what came to be known as the "Green Line"—a street that ran in a straight line from the National Museum down to Martyrs Square in the center of Beirut. The AUB Medical Center (AUBMC) was part of the University complex, which was located in the western sector, about 750 meters from the large hotels, where some of the first and fiercest battles erupted. There were four other major medical facilities in the western sector: the Barbir Hospital, the Makassed General Hospital, the Arab University Hospital and the Beirut General Hospital. All five hospitals together received and treated the casualties that came in from the western sector of the city and its outskirts; but because AUBMC was the largest of all (420 beds) and was also a teaching center, it received the most casualties. In addition, its emergency unit never closed its doors, unlike others that did so to avoid taking in more casualties than they could treat.

Throughout the summer of 1975, the news on the radio (most newspapers had ceased publishing) reflected the escalation of conflict in the country. Electricity and water services went completely out in most of West Beirut; but AUB had its own generators and water sources and in many respects could continue to function

American University of Beirut Medical Center: violence and destruction at AUBMC's doors

normally. Throughout the city, however, people became more and more frightened and began preparing themselves for the long haul—stocking up on food, installing battery-operated lights or generators, storing water and digging wells. Garbage began piling up on the streets in huge, unhealthy mounds and at night the city was pitch black except for the fireworks of shells and artillery that lit up the sky.

In December, Dean Robert Najemy, an American of Lebanese origin who was the Dean of Students, telephoned to tell us to evacuate Building 56. There were gunmen shouting and shooting all around the Medical Gate (one of the entrances to the University) and in front of the women's dormitories: Murex, Bustani, Jewett and Building 56. At the Murex dorm, the gunmen forced themselves in, demanded identification cards and want-

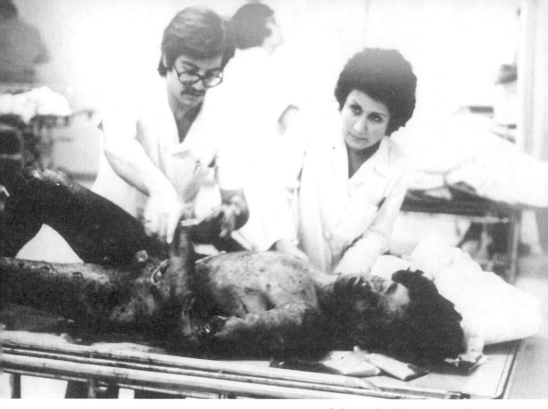

Saving a patient in the emergency unit

ed to check every room. Rough and rude, with wild beards and bulging eyes that looked as though they were drugged, they pushed the terrified women around. Fortunately, the University's security guards were able to negotiate the gunmen's withdrawal without serious harm to the women, except for the psychological trauma.

This was six months before I was supposed to graduate, and I had been eagerly looking forward to that day in June 1976 when I would walk up to the podium in cap and gown to receive my degree and become a full-fledged nurse. That dream, however, soon faded when we learned that commencement exercises would be cancelled and we would be receiving our diplomas without any ceremony whatsoever. I had promised my brother George that I would leave Lebanon after graduation, and now the threatening prospect of a long, raging war gave me every reason to do so. We kept hearing all kinds of rumors and everyone was frightened, sensing there would be many bad days ahead, but no one really knew what was going to happen and for how long and why. Those who could afford it began leaving the country in droves; others moved out of the city to safer mountain areas. But many of us at AUB, naively believing it would remain a safe haven against assault, stayed on.

## Chapter Three
# Security Deteriorates

By February 1976, Beirut had fallen into total chaos. The protective assurances of normal law and order had evaporated, and we at AUB began to feel the ominous threat of uncontrolled mayhem seep into campus life. Many students, agitated and emboldened by the atmosphere of war, began harassing and even threatening members of the administration and faculty over differences in political affiliation and, more dangerously, over dissatisfaction with the grades they received. Stoking the fire was the angry presence around campus of several students who had been expelled from AUB during the strikes and sit-ins of 1973 and whose petitions for re-admission had been denied.

On the morning of February 17, one of these expelled students—whether in a psychotic rage or coldly in calculated revenge—somehow got onto the AUB campus and went on a shooting spree. His first target was the Dean of the Faculty of Engineering, Ray Ghosn. He simply marched into the Dean's office and shot him dead. He

Shell damage to one
of the nurse's rooms

then ran up the hill and at gunpoint forced himself into the office of Dean Najemy and also shot him. His third stop was College Hall, where he took several AUB officials hostage, including Vice President George Hakim, and where he was finally talked into surrendering. The young student was subsequently convicted, sentenced and jailed, but when the conditions of war forced the closure of Lebanon's prisons, he was released along with all other prisoners. He is now free.

Dean Najemy's wife happened to be a patient in my care on that dark day of madness. She had been admitted to the AUBMC for lower back pain. As news of the shootings on campus began circulating through the hospital and we learned that Dean Najemy had been brought to the Emergency Unit and had died there, Mrs. Najemy sensed something was wrong and asked me what the commotion was all about. I simply did not know what to say to her. How could I, a student nurse in an apricot uniform, tell the wife of the Dean of Students that her husband had been murdered? I was saved from this painful prospect by the sudden arrival in the room of a group of AUB officials led by President Samuel Kirkwood, Dean of the Medical School Dr. Samuel Asper, and AUBMC Director Munther Kuzayli. There was no need for words; the expression on their faces confirmed her worst fears.

It was my first experience as a nurse comforting someone who had just lost a loved one. After the men had left and she burst out with heart-rending cries of, "Why? Why? Why?" I spontaneously put my arms around her and held her close, wanting my embrace to comfort and convey what no words could express.

This was our deadly introduction to the beginning of rule by the gun. As the weeks and months passed and I volunteered on emergency units, I saw many more victims of gunshot wounds. It was as if Beirut had gone totally mad. We seldom knew who was fighting whom, nor was this our concern. All we knew and cared about was saving lives.

Towards the end of April, a general ceasefire of ten days gave many of the hospital staff a chance to leave the hospital. One after another, they bundled up their families and moved to the safety of villages in the mountains. They left from all departments—nursing, pharmacy, central supply, dietary, housekeeping, plant engineering. Some even left the country, including physicians, surgeons and other specialized professionals. For those who remained at their posts, the days became a continuous pattern of non-stop work.

The divided city made it extremely difficult for the AUBMC nurses living in East Beirut to get to work. They were forced to stop at militia checkpoints all along the way. On several occasions, the van transporting them was hijacked and its occupants left stranded on the road. Once, when the AUB mini-bus was returning the nurses to their homes in East Beirut, a jeep full of militiamen intercepted the bus at gunpoint and took the driver hostage. They then proceeded to move its occupants around like checkers in a game. They drove the bus into a gas station, where they ordered the male Christians to get out, then told all the female occupants to step down. The women refused, and after an hour of touch-and-go negotiations with the militia leader (much of it conducted by the women), the driver was released and the bus, with all its occupants back on board, was left to proceed on its way. (Interestingly, war or no war, women in Lebanon usually are handled with a chivalrous respect that is inbred in Arab males. We rarely heard of the molestation

or rape of women during the entire fifteen years of war.)
The next day, we discovered that all the gunmen wanted
was the bus itself. That night, after delivering all the nurses
to their homes, the AUB driver was again stopped and
forced out, but this time the bus was irrevocably hijacked.

The Museum Green Line would close and open
depending on the battle situation. Crossing it was like
running an obstacle course. It meant walking (often
loaded down with baggage), stopping at each checkpoint
to show identification, watching out for snipers on the
way, moving fast in between sudden waves of shelling.
There was another road that led to East Beirut, called the
Saint Franciscan, which was used when the Museum road
was closed. It was an old horse track, full of hard-to-walk-
on red sand that had been used to exercise racehorses.
Only army or government vehicles or those with special
permission were allowed to cross. It was always a scary
trip, but for those living on one side, with jobs, family or
other commitments on the other, it was unavoidable and,
in time, it became a routine. Later, when all cars were
allowed to cross, it took six hours to make a trip that
normally took ten minutes, because of the slowdown of
traffic at the many checkpoints.

Many of the young, during this first year of the war,
went out of control. Some of them became dangerously
reckless, moving around during the thick of battles and
challenging each other in playing a Lebanese version of
Russian roulette. In one six-month period, six teenagers
who had lost out in the game were admitted to AUBMC
with shotgun wounds in the head. They all died. One of
them was followed by his best friend the next day. It seems
the girlfriend of the first had asked the friend, "How did
he die?" Whereupon, the friend picked up a gun, pointed
it at his head and said, "Like this." He too failed to draw a

blank and died. Children of six or seven strutted around, carrying guns as though they were characters in a cowboy or police movie. Youths ran through sniper-filled streets in a game that they often lost of dodging bullets. It was all so very, very insane and sad.

As counselor of Building 56, I took care of arranging housing for those nurses who decided to remain and live on campus. This posed no problem, since all classes at the University had been suspended in February and many students had left for home, which left many dorm rooms empty. For the graduating seniors of nursing, however, classes resumed in April. Esther Moyer, director of the School of Nursing, was determined that we continue our studies and not delay our graduation. The hospital needed more full-fledged nurses and this was one way to get them, she reasoned. The classes were held in Building 56, where we were all housed. And the tunnel leading to the hospital gave us safe access to its cafeteria, where we had our daily meals. Some students, psychologically stressed by the constant pressures of war, balked at continuing with their studies. But against all odds, we finished our courses and completed all requirements for graduation.

As May approached, the fighting increased. On one day alone, 220 casualties were brought into the Emergency Unit. We all ran there to help and all we could see were dead bodies, simply identified as Unknown I, II, III and so on, strewn across the floor and piled one on top of the other. As a student there was not much I could do except take care of minor tasks like cleaning up and running for medical supplies. The doctors and nurses had no time to instruct or explain, but I just could not stand there and watch. So I tried to anticipate their needs and somehow or other, I think my presence made a difference.

As the tension in Lebanon grew, we in Building 56 also became tenser. Our graduation day was approaching; and although AUB was a relatively safe haven, we knew there would be no graduation ceremony, no cap and gown. What we did not know, however, was that before then we would be given a firsthand taste of war in all its mechanized powers of destruction.

On June 8, 1976, at around midnight, a huge shell shot through the sky from East Beirut and landed in our building through the kitchen on the fifth floor. Fortunately, there were no bedrooms on this floor. I was still awake reading in bed, unable to sleep, when the thunderous sound of metal piercing cement and stone hit my ears. I had never heard such a sound before, but I would hear it again and again every time the fighting intensified.

Without thinking twice, I jumped out of bed, put on my robe, grabbed the master key, rushed out of my room and ran downstairs to open the entrance door of the building. My only thought was to lead my student charges out of the building and through the tunnel into the safety of the hospital. My legs were shaking and I was afraid of further shelling—we had been warned that a second and third shell usually followed in the same path as the first. I was not experienced in disaster planning, but knew enough to check every room to make sure no one was hurt. I was alone with the head resident who was my senior.

There were around 100 women in the building and, as I checked every room, their terrified screaming echoed through the halls. One of them, pale and shaken, called out to me in a pleading voice, "Gladys, I'm hurt; please help me." Her injury turned out to be minor and self-inflicted. She had panicked and fallen while running down the stairs. This same student later went into a severe depression and committed suicide. No longer able to cope, she went up to the tenth floor of the hospital and threw herself off.

Some of the women, immobilized and in a state of shock, refused to leave the building. And while others ran down in their pajamas or nightgowns, I compulsively went back to my room and changed into proper clothing. This would always be my reaction in times of heavy shelling. I just did not want to end up in the Emergency Unit in my nightgown. When one of the students rushed up to me screaming, "My room has been hit," and I saw the huge hole in the wall, I too started to panic. Fortunately, at that moment, Dr. Asper arrived, and with him were Hajj Omar Faour, the man in charge of AUB's motor pool, and Donald Meyer, Comptroller of the University. We were without electricity and all were carrying flashlights.

Fortified by this male contingent of moral support, I proceeded to open every room to make sure all the students had left the building, that there was not some poor soul lying in a corner somewhere wounded or dead. As we moved up the stairs and then descended, floor by floor, we were shocked by the extent of the damage. On the fifth floor, the shell had made a hole through half the wall; on the fourth, there was a second huge hole through the floor. The shell had then travelled down through the third and second floors, leaving a trail of gaping holes behind, until it finally reached the first floor. There it exploded in the Nursing School's laboratory and, in a final spurt of energy, flew out of the building and into the garden. Do not ask me how all this happened, but it did. It was what I saw, witnessed and photographed.

All the students were gathered in the tunnel, some sleepy, some crying, some homesick, some stunned, some frightened. Slowly, everyone calmed down, but we all knew we would be spending the rest of the night in our "bomb shelter." There would be no going back to our rooms except to quickly pick up whatever we needed to make ourselves more comfortable.

We did not get back to our quarters in Building 56 for the next several days, until holes were patched, windows replaced and the debris cleaned up. We moved into the Sabbagh Basic Medical Sciences Building, into its huge underground floor, which was large enough to accommodate all the residents of the four women's dorms. Some of us still had to study and prepare for our finals. Some played the guitar, others played cards, and others just sat crying. We spent a lot of time talking to each other, recalling a peaceful past, wondering about our future, consol-

Asleep in the tunnel, safe from the shelling

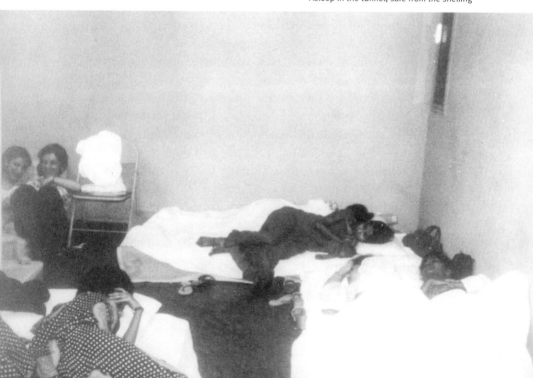

ing those who were scared and depressed.

Night after night we slept on the floor without mattresses, but fortunately, with blankets, which were in short supply. It was uncomfortable, but we adapted and tried to function as normally as possible by playing tennis, participating in campus life, and shopping for food. The weather was so beautiful and we enjoyed the imposed, tight-quartered camaraderie, yet it was all so very sad.

The following week, as the situation continued to worsen, the airport closed down, and on June 15, when the students went on strike, AUB closed. On June 18 U.S. Ambassador Francis E. Meloy was assassinated. The U.S. Embassy advised all Americans to leave Lebanon and announced arrangements for an "organized departure." I was confused and did not know what to do. I had graduated—without ceremony, of course—and was now secure in a profession that could take me anywhere. Yet, I was unable to decide whether to go or stay. I was twenty years old.

Day by day the hospital kept receiving more and more casualties and inadequate staffing became a serious problem. Some got burnt out and could no longer function; others simply left. Many nurses lived at AUB, unable to go home for months at a time. The hospital became home to them and the patients and staff became their family. They worked long hard hours receiving many critical patients and often sleeping at their units; yet when off duty they could still laugh and share meals and play cards together. Each unit, in a way, became one big family—separate families in separate units away from their true families.

As a student, I had learned how much good nursing depended on devotion and commitment, on assuming total responsibility towards the institution and its patients. Some lost that sense of devotion and commitment, were able to detach themselves from moral responsibility, and left. In others, like myself, the feeling of responsibility grew with every terrible passing day. We believed so strongly in what we were doing, in the vital difference that our staying would mean. For me, it was also a personal challenge, born perhaps out of an innate refusal to ever submit to defeat—I wanted to prove to myself and to others that I could survive. And as the years went by, that challenge became an obsession that almost killed me.

Living conditions throughout the city became increasingly difficult. Cars were constantly stolen, sometimes with their drivers. Houses, whose owners dared to leave them unprotected by one militia or another, were occupied by force. Telephone lines were cut, electricity became sporadic, and the city began facing a serious shortage of water. With ingenious skill, however, the creative and resourceful Lebanese came up with a quick solution to every problem. They dug wells for water (brackish and salty, but still water); installed electric generators everywhere; strung up their own telephone lines to replace those cut and, neighborhood by neighborhood, pooled all their resources to keep themselves supplied with basic needs. By then, of course, a black market, stocked with a wide variety of consumer goods, was firmly established and flourishing.

Life on the AUB campus was somewhat easier. The raging sea of war that rose and fell beyond our walls, however, battered at the resistance of every person living in the city. As I look back on those years, I still wonder how the Lebanese coped, how so many of them never gave up, how after every blow they could bounce back so quickly. I do not think there is another population in the entire world that could have done the same.

From its inception, AUBMC was dedicated to excellence in teaching and services and, under normal conditions, these twins of academic and medical concerns remained superior and inseparable. However, the overwhelming strain of that first year of the civil war seriously impaired the hospital's capacity to cope with the large numbers of casualties that poured into its Emergency Unit, and gradually its standards began to suffer. One of the first casualties was in the teaching of medical and nursing students. Teaching could not be limited to the "trauma" medicine that our students were daily and almost exclusively exposed to. In addition, our educational links with the outside world had been essentially severed—which meant no medical or nursing journals, no visiting lecturers, no new equipment or teaching tools. By June 1976, most of the teaching had come to a standstill and we soon realized that the fighting would drag on for many months to come—but still not even imagining that it would go on for years to come.

In effect, AUBMC became a military field hospital. More than ninety percent of the patient population were war casualties suffering from multiple injuries. Because of the intense urgent demand for hospital beds, all admissions for elective medical care were refused; and while surgical admissions rose sharply, other services suffered. The civil war crept up on us from all sides. There was the brain drain, the sudden exodus of some of our most qualified people. The resident staff was reduced by at least fifty percent and nurses were called upon to assume some of their duties (within limits). The attending staff, meanwhile, was reduced by at least sixty to seventy percent, as was the nursing staff.

In the Department of Surgery, which became the hub of activity at the hospital, only eight of twenty-two

attending surgeons (about thirty-five percent) remained and only two to three out of ten operating suites were in service. This shortage came at a time when the number of surgical patients had almost quadrupled.

The dangers and difficulties of crossing from one section of the city to the other—across the "front lines," so to speak—caused a daily absence of staff, as well as the permanent departure of some. Nurses, physicians and other hospital personnel who happened to live in East Beirut and had to cross through the lines to get to the hospital in West Beirut were frequently stopped and had to argue their way through. The key argument, of course, was that they were taking care of war casualties, irrespective of religion, and that it was to the advantage of all that they be permitted to pass through and get to the hospital.

The Intensive Care Unit finally had to close due to lack of staff and its patients were moved into the Recovery Unit, where a more careful triage (or priority scale) was applied to decide on treatment priorities. From the beginning of the war in April 1975 to November 1976, the AUBMC Emergency Unit received 8,326 casualties; 1,882 were admitted and 429 were dead on arrival.

Both patients and staff felt the impact of shortages on the services. Many departments came to a complete standstill. The computer center totally broke down, which meant that among other things, bills could not be prepared. The Emergency Unit became so crowded that it could no longer adequately receive patients. By May, the hospital administration realized it could no longer continue its open-door policy of admitting every patient brought to its Emergency Unit. If it expected to continue operating, AUBMC had to initiate a more selective admissions approach. The new policy adopted limited emergency admissions to any one of the following conditions:

Hoarding water wherever it could be found

31

1) intracranial injuries; 2) thoracic and cardiovascular injuries; 3) peripheral vascular injuries; 4) complicated injuries of the limbs requiring major bone and soft tissue reconstruction; and 5) patients in shock and non-transferable due to multiple injuries.

Despite the policy, we still encountered problems in limiting admissions. Moreover, once patients were admitted, it was often very difficult to discharge them when treatment was completed. Some of them had lost their homes and families and had no one to care for them. They wanted to remain in the hospital, safe and well-fed.

I, meanwhile, was wrestling with my own problem. I had indeed graduated and I kept thinking about my promise to my brother that I would leave Lebanon as soon as I graduated. Yet all that I had experienced during the past year was still so vivid in my mind, so real, that it was as though no other world existed for me outside of AUB. Many of the memories were good—the dear friendships nurtured by adversity and human kindness; the simple, pure pleasures of living on a paradisiacal slope next to a brilliant blue sea; the daily gratification of knowing that in one way or another my work as a nurse had eased pain and brought comfort to people.

Other memories were not so good, but they stayed with me and still keep me captive, almost like the phantom presence of a lost limb. These are memories I can never forget. I remember the sight of bodies one day—more than 140 of them—piled up one on top of the other, brought into the Emergency Unit from a bombed out cinema. It happened so suddenly. We heard the sound of sirens, horns blaring, militiamen shouting and firing their guns in the air to clear the way, family relatives of the wounded crowding behind them. With the force of an uncontrollable mob, they stormed into the Emergency Unit, shouting and screaming

Stretchers waiting for casualties in front of AUBMC

for immediate attention, carrying bodies and forcibly pushing their way in. In two minutes, the entire Emergency Unit was jammed with people.

I stood there in the corridor, scared, shivering and staring at the horrible scene before me. I saw legs and arms and organs hanging from bodies or totally cut off and carried in by someone else—as though, by some magic, the human flesh and bones that had been blown apart could be pasted together again. I stood there, coughing from the stench of burnt flesh, my eyes burning. I wanted to run away, but I stayed and however I could I tried to help.

Everywhere there were children, either dead or alive. I remember seeing the intestines of a child spilling out and watching an intern slowly trying to put them back in again. I remember a dead woman,

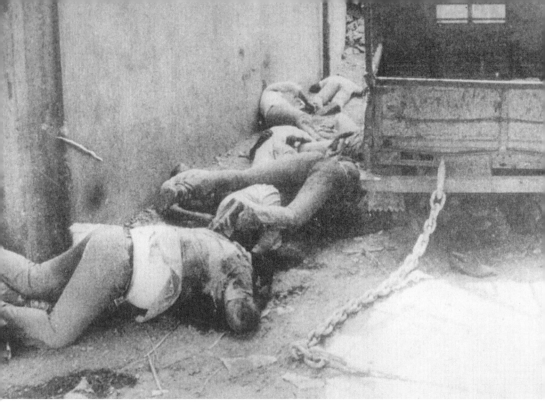

The deadly human cost of war accumulated in an alley

her brain blown to pieces, and the little girl holding her hand, crying, "Mommy, wake up! I want to go home. I'm hungry." I took her in my arms and hugged her tightly, then took her to the Office of Nursing Services to look after her and try to find her father or some other member of her family.

Both the good and the bad make up a life. And in three short but very concentrated years, Lebanon and AUBMC had become my life. I thought long and hard before I decided to listen to my brother and leave Lebanon and pursue my future in the U.S. The airport was closed, so I arranged to go overland to Damascus and take a plane from there. I would be travelling with another nurse who was leaving to join her fiancé in the U.S. But on June 22, 1976, two days before our departure, she was killed by a mortar shell while walking home from the hospital. She had just finished her shift and had said goodbye to all her friends and patients. She was wearing her white uniform. She was twenty-three years old.

This tragic event marked my farewell to Lebanon. It took eight hours to make the overland trip to Damascus, which would normally take no more than three hours. We had to pass through sixty-five militia and army road-blocks, where it certainly helped to have an American passport—it was accorded full respect and no questions were asked. I was not to have that same sense of security as an American in Lebanon when I returned several months later.

To be back in the U.S. was both strange and exciting. Suddenly, Lebanon seemed so far away, as though all that I had lived through there was a dream. Soon after I arrived in Rhode Island, where my brother lived, I was interviewed by the local newspaper and asked about my experiences in Lebanon. One of the first questions put to me was whether the war in Lebanon was a religious one between Christians and Moslems. My immediate response, of course, was that it was not, that behind the civil war were many political issues that had to do more with the larger regional conflict than with internal animosities in Lebanon. I stressed that religion was used as a convenient excuse and that I lived in an area of Beirut where the population was a mixture of both Christians and Moslems, living side by side as neighbors and daily helping each other through difficulties.

After passing my state board exams as a nurse in November 1976, I started working at the Rhode Island Hospital. But as the months went by, the yearning to return to Lebanon remained constantly in my thoughts. Adding fuel to the fire of my desire were the communications I kept receiving from friends in Lebanon urging me to return—especially from Dr. Asper and from Sheila Hammond, a British nurse who was Director of Nursing Services. I finally reached the point of firm decision; and in April 1978, despite my brother's objections, I packed my bags and boarded a plane for Beirut.

Initially, it was not easy re-adapting to life in Beirut, to the lack of those basic services, such as adequate water, electricity and telephones, which are taken so much for granted in the U.S. and many other countries. My very first assignment at the hospital turned out to be Ward 5 South, a challenging medical unit of thirty-eight patients, all poor but so very appreciative of every little thing we did for them. They literally looked upon us as their saviors and kept showering us with gifts—all modest, certainly, but offered with intense expressions of gratitude. Family members would bring in vegetables, fruits, and sweets, whatever they had at home or on the farm. I will never forget the day when one patient's father, a farmer, brought me a live chicken, eggs, vegetables and potatoes all loaded in a big crate.

I grew to love these patients and spent many late hours in the ward caring for and comforting them. By then, I had learned basic conversational Arabic and was able to communicate with them in their language. This was of immeasurable help not only in handling their physical needs but also in strengthening the human bonds between us. People were getting more and more depressed over the war and being a helpless patient lying in a hospital bed while all hell was breaking loose outside was not easy. Often, more than medication, they needed our moral support.

Eight months later, I was promoted to the position of Head Nurse of 5 South. By then, the Director of Nursing, Sheila Hammond, had left AUBMC and returned to her home in Belfast, where she was decorated by Queen Elizabeth for all her services to the Lebanese people.

In December 1976, while I was gone, a group of seventeen volunteer U.S. Public Health Service nurses had been sent to work at AUBMC for a period of sixty days. Seven of them later requested a thirty-day extension of their assignment, which enabled the hospital to reopen its Intensive Care Unit.

In February 1977, a rehabilitation program for limb prosthetics was established at AUBMC and other medical centers. During that month, a prosthetics expert from the Netherlands examined a total of 420 amputees. Measurements were taken and in March a group of Dutch technicians arrived to prepare the preliminary plaster molds to be used in making the prosthesis casts in Holland. The final phase of the program began in mid-April, when a team of some twenty Dutch technicians arrived in Beirut with the casts and outfitted all the amputees.

That same year AUBMC also became handicapped by an acute shortage of nurses, exacerbated both by the steady departure of those who could not take it anymore and by the phasing out of the Diploma Nursing Program in 1976. As a consequence, two medical/surgical units of thirty beds each (8 North and 8 South) were closed and the Intensive Care Unit was left with only four beds. A new request for foreign volunteers in April helped ease the shortage.

Doo

Leb

in t

H

DO NOT LEAVE YOUR COUNTR

IO NOT LEAVE YOUR COUNTRY

ors,

non is

rmoil ...

ELP !

WHEN IT HELPS US.

EEDS YOU.    MSS.

## Chapter Four

# The Israeli Invasion

In 1981, I was appointed to the challenging position of Nursing Supervisor of all medical units. While I welcomed the recognition bestowed upon me by the promotion, I missed my patients in 5 South and, to this day, I can honestly say that my nursing experience on that ward was one of the most gratifying of my career. There is nothing that can equal the deep satisfaction of providing direct patient care, and this personal fulfillment becomes less and less as one moves up the ladder of management. It is true that in management, one has a greater impact on decision-making, on bringing about changes of wide benefit, but how much more rewarding it is to look into the grateful eyes of a patient you have cared for through the dark hours of a life-threatening illness or injury. I still miss those days of direct patient care.

I often dreamed of my patients at night and it was difficult to hold back the tears when one of them died. Slowly, I learned how to cope with patients in crisis. My strategy of dealing with such situations revolved around

Israeli bombing rains more death on Beirut

what I would call the ABCs of emergency response: stay calm, think and act. It was important not to show alarm and, in turn, alarm everyone around you. Sometimes, in order to turn my attention to sudden, more urgent demands, I would delegate responsibilities to others, to those I knew could handle them. The most important thing was to avoid panic. This early experience in handling crises was of enormous help to me later when I was faced with emergencies on a much larger scale.

As a supervisor, I had to assume a different role and "play nurse" to a different class of "patients" belonging to a different "unit" in the hospital. I had to deal with all kinds of problems on a daily basis, many of them stemming from the war situation and not usually found in the "job description" of a nursing supervisor. I had to shore up the persistent shortage of staff throughout the three-shift, twenty-four-hour hospital workday, caused by the irregular attendance of employees. I spent precious time repairing breakdowns in interpersonal relationships among staff members, figuring out how to replenish supply shortages, and alleviating symptoms of stress and burnout among my staff members.

As with my patients in 5 South, I had to turn a sensitive listening ear to my nurses—those who had family problems, those who could not get to work because of the fighting, those who could not sleep at night because of the shelling. The attendance of nurses living in East Beirut, of course, was most erratic. Most of them were Christians and they were afraid to come to the largely Moslem west side of Beirut where AUB is located, afraid of being harassed or even assaulted by Moslem militias. And the same fears were felt by Moslems who for one reason or another—work, family or friends—had to cross over to East Beirut. Handling this potentially explosive source of conflict among the staff—which was a mix of Moslems and Christians—called for very delicate handling, and I had to always make sure to never, never take sides. It was not easy, but with caution and the good will of neutrality, I managed to avoid disaster more than once.

Meanwhile, we all tried to retain some semblance of normalcy in our lives. During one relatively calm period, a group of the nurses who worked with me decided to put on a comedy show they had written called "The Nursing Syndrome." These nurses, who were loyal, motivated and devoted to their profession, also proved to have a great sense of humor. The hilarious interpretation they gave of the hospital's activities did much to vent our frustrations. One scene involved a visit to AUBMC by the U.S. Joint Commission on Accreditation of Hospitals. With the sound of shells exploding in the background, the Commission's inspection team walks through the hospital picking on small details of administration, sternly asking, for instance: "Where is your documentation? If you did not document the care, you did not perform it!"

Years before, AUBMC had been accredited by the Joint Commission and was one of only three hospitals outside the U.S. holding this accreditation. Since then, every three years, a survey team had been coming out to re-assess the hospital's accreditation, until the travel advisory and ban on Americans travelling to Lebanon was imposed.

Another amusing scene had a group of soldiers speaking Hebrew and forcing themselves into a patient's room when suddenly there's a power failure and the lights go out. In the darkness the nurse mistakenly gives medication to one of the patient's visitors; then, realizing her mistake, makes him spit it out and turns around and gives it to the patient. All we got to see, however, were the rehearsals. Ironically, performance of the show was interrupted by the Israeli invasion.

This totally different kind of war, of one country attacking another, all started on June 6, 1982. It brought us high-flying aircraft dropping bombs on civilian targets, low-flying planes strafing byways and highways. It meant a brutal invasion by foot soldiers, tanks and other armored vehicles that swept straight up the coast of Lebanon and into Beirut. It was not East against West or Christian against Moslem; it was not one local militia against another. It was Israel against Lebanon. The civil war had now become an international war.

This kind of war was the scariest of all. In the civil conflict we had been experiencing, we always had a hunch when the shooting or shelling would start. Reliable rumors would fly through the city, or there would be a public threat from one militia to another, or suddenly some political figure would be assassinated—and the fighting would start up again. But in this country-against-country conflict, only the combatants themselves knew when, where and how. It was, in every way, a different kind of war, in which all the Lebanese felt united against one enemy. It felt good to be united and this spirit invaded the hospital. In all the years of the war, this was the only time that everyone in the hospital worked and volunteered without complaint, without political animosity and with non-stop commitment.

Needless to say, my brother George was extremely worried about me—and very angry about what was happening to Lebanon, so much so that he wrote the following letter to the Los Angeles Times:

I have a sister who is a nurse at the American University Hospital in West Beirut. I'm enclosing her letter dated June 18, 1982, received through one of the Americans who was evacuated. I want you to see the situation from an uncensored source. The devastation and indiscriminate killing is unprecedented in today's civilized world.

Last night, July 7, 1982, after 30 straight days of trying to call Beirut, I finally got through and spoke with my sister. The situation is worse than I expected. Contrary to this morning's papers, the water supply has not been restored. Many of the foreign nurses left after the shelling started. My sister and the other nurses are working two shifts a day to keep up with the incoming casualties. Although the city has no power, the hospital has a two-week supply of fuel to run the generators and maintain electricity.

She has gone through the civil war of 1976; however, this is ten times worse. There were no air raids in 1976. She is scared and terrified. People are unable to sleep during the night due to the shelling and flares that keep up the psychological pressure. The tension is nerve-wracking and the psychological damage will continue for a long time. Although my sister is American, she has elected to stay in West Beirut and help where she is badly needed. She and her Lebanese colleagues cannot comprehend why the world, and especially the United States, is doing nothing about the Israelis, who are holding up medical supplies to West Beirut, continuing the indiscriminate bombing, using internationally-outlawed cluster and phosphorus bombs, and causing shortages of necessities to 600,000 civilians.

I ask the people of the United States: Is this justified; where is the outrage, where is your conscience, why have you not demanded of your leaders to stop this monstrous Israeli machine immediately? What is it going to take to wake you up to what is going on? Maybe the inevitable blood bath that will take place when the Israelis go into West Beirut!

My brother, unlike me, had strong political views on the Israeli-Palestinian conflict, which he had often expressed to me. I knew little about politics and the reasons for the conflict with Israel. I only knew from Palestinian friends that they had a just cause and wanted to return to their country, Palestine. There were many Palestinians in Lebanon and we had a number of Palestinian doctors, nurses and other employees in the hospital, who were all hard workers and had stuck it through the worst of times.

At that point, however, it did not interest me why the conflict had erupted. I had other things to worry about, such as getting my work done and surviving. Then one day in that horrendous month of June, we heard the radio flash a report that the Israeli Army had invaded South Lebanon and was moving north. A state of alert was announced and the entire city came to a standstill; schools closed and people panicked, especially those who had families in the south. At the hospital, most of our orderlies, nurses and aides were from the south and they fell into a frenzy of concern for their families. We were all worried and very agitated, not knowing what would happen next.

The air raids were devastating—there was nowhere to hide in this kind of warfare. Those who have lived through the World War bombardments of cities will know how we felt. The Israelis had not yet invaded Beirut, but everyone knew it was bound to happen. Most of the Palestinians were in West Beirut and we at AUB found ourselves inescapably caught in the middle. The hospital, of course, would be involved in coping with the consequences and we had to prepare for the day when casualties would begin pouring into the Emergency Unit.

In an attempt to make up for the severe shortage of staff, a Volunteer's Office was established in coordination with the Office of Nursing Services. It was the brainstorm idea of Chris Weir, an RN and the daughter of Reverend Benjamin Weir, who was later kidnapped. Volunteers were needed at all levels in all departments, especially in nursing. Almost everyone wanted to leave when the air raids started, and we hardly had enough manpower to keep the hospital going.

The call for volunteers was gratifying and we immediately put them through quick intensive training in handling specific areas of hospital work. The volunteers and the duties they were assigned fell into four different categories:

*Third and Fourth-Year Nursing Students*: These volunteers were not many in number, but they filled an essential need. They functioned as staff nurses and were assigned to units according to their capabilities. They could administer medications and perform many routine nursing procedures.

*Medicine I and II Students and Associate Nursing Degree Students*: After receiving a brief course in basic nursing care, these students were assigned to serve as aides, orderlies or

Terrorized Beirut residents flee the air raids

transport assistants. They could provide basic care, such as taking and recording blood pressure, pulse rates and temperature; they could make beds, give baths or back rubs, feed and transport patients.

*Medicine III Students*: Capable of providing more advanced nursing care because of their training, these volunteers were assigned as assistants to the RNs. They could handle the monitor in the Coronary Care Unit and watch for arrhythmias. They could also draw blood samples, insert infusions, change dressings and prescribe emergency medications. The experience gave many of them valuable insight into the many-faceted role of the nurse and later helped them as resident doctors to understand the value of nurse-doctor teamwork in providing good medical care.

*Non-medical Volunteers*: This group included other AUB students who were housed in campus dorms because they could not get home when the University temporarily closed, as well as faculty and members of their families who were living on campus. It was a mixed batch of helping hands, young and old, but all were put to work in one way or another.

Out of these categories—which represented different age groups, different levels of education and different backgrounds—emerged a reliable team of highly motivated volunteers that soon proved to be an invaluable asset to the hospital. Without doubt, a vital element in the project's success was Chris Weir, who served as head of the Volunteer Office. I was in continuous contact with her and daily saw what an impact her dynamic energy and sense of commitment had on the people around her.

Shift schedules were set up weekly, and every Monday volunteers would check in for their assignments. Working in coordination with the Nursing Services (of which I was a supervisor at the time), the Volunteer Office would provide volunteers according to need, but would always try to get the same people lined up for the same work in the same place. We found it more efficient to centralize the assignment process in the Office of Nursing Services. Each area or unit of the hospital—such as Pharmacy, Dietary, Central Supply, Housekeeping and so on—would call in and make its request and we, in turn, would confer with the Volunteer Office in making assignments according to the capabilities of the volunteers available at the time.

In June 1982, 159 volunteers worked a total of 673 days, at an average number of 4.2 days and a maximum of 16 days. In the following month of July, 128 volunteers worked a total of 1,037 days, at an average of 9.5 days and a maximum of 27 days. An on-call list, including telephone numbers and shift preference, was created for each category of volunteers. We also received the help of nurses from nearby small hospitals that had closed because of lack of staff.

Volunteer help, of course, had its disadvantages. Many, especially in the non-medical category, were people who knew absolutely nothing about the working environment of a hospital and had to be trained. But there was no time (or staff) to give them more than a two-day orientation: the first day on patient care, such as distributing meal trays, feeding patients, providing moral support; and the second day on the duties of a unit clerk or receptionist, such as answering the phones, paging doctors and nurses, directing visitors. After that, they were on their own to learn whatever else they needed to know on the job.

At the time, I was the only day supervisor of nursing left. In fact, there were only four nursing supervisors left to serve the entire hospital twenty-four hours a day, seven days a week. We had almost no free time and it was not easy. We had to tour every unit of the hospital every day to check the casualties, lend support to the staff and make sure that everything was functioning as it should. Because there were not enough head nurses to run the units, the staff often felt insecure and needed constant reassurance. The Philippine nurses recruited in 1978 to make up for the nursing shortage had never experienced such a war situation before and were especially scared.

The hospital was tested in many other ways that year. It was not enough that we had to cope with the heavy load of casualties and the severe shortage of staff. We also had to deal with some non-medical problems as well. People— especially those living in the Palestinian refugee camp areas targeted by Israel's bombs—would come to visit patients and, finding the hospital a very safe and comfortable haven, would decide to stay. Why not? The hospital, after all, had electricity, water and food. And, above all, it provided the safest shelter in Beirut; certainly the Israelis would not bomb an American institution. There was nothing we could do about it. Some slept in the rooms of the patients they came to visit; others camped out in stairwells and around the entrance to the hospital.

I will never forget the morning I walked through the tunnel from Building 56 and found people lying there side by side. I was in my white uniform and cap, rushing to my 7:00 a.m. shift after a more or less calm night, when I tripped over a pair of legs and almost landed on top of the body they belonged to. I looked down and saw the pain-wracked face of an old man. He looked up at me with a sigh of relief, as though I were an angel of mercy who had sud-denly appeared from heaven. He was so thin, so old and frail, and so apologetic in his apparent need to talk to me. I told him I had to go to work, but he begged me to stay with him "for five minutes" and began to tell me about the one room he had lived in that was destroyed and how alone in the world he now was, with little food and no one to help him. He told me how he used to sell cigarettes along the streets from a pushcart that also was gone. And he told me about his medical problems.

How could I help him, how could I tell him I would take care of him? In my dorm? In the hospital? All I could do was run back to my room, gather together some food and money and bring my offering back to him. His name was Hassan. And for many days and nights afterwards, I kept seeing the soft, smiling, aching face of this man whose life would surely end in sorrow.

Most of the people in the tunnel were Palestinians who had fled the camps and sought refuge there from the heavy Israeli shelling. The invasion of the hospital by these poor souls soon reached a troubling peak that began to interfere with the hospital's activities. Something had to be done about their presence. Pushed to the limits of its capabilities and endurance, the hospital could no longer afford this chaotic intrusion. Finally, to the great relief of the hospital staff, AUBMC officials were able to get the PLO to issue an order to all Palestinians occupying the hospital to vacate the premises immediately.

As the nursing shortage continued to worsen, the hospital had to depend more and more on volunteer help. From June 6 to September 10, 1982, the AUBMC staff experienced an absentee rate of sixty-seven percent in registered nurses, sixty percent in practical nurses, sixty percent in unit clerks and seventy percent in nurse's aides. The hospital census in 1982 was 344 beds occupied, compared with 318 in 1976. As a result of the nursing shortage and the increased census, we had to close units that had become a luxury we could no longer afford.

On June 7, 1982, the Cardiac Surgery Unit closed. To perform elective heart surgery, with casualties pouring in and adding to an already high infection rate, had now become an unacceptable risk. On June 24, the Private

Pediatric Unit of twenty-five beds also closed—few parents were ready to put their children in a hospital except for emergency care. One after another, units providing the normal surgical and medical services that represent the bulk of most hospital care came to a standstill. On June 24, one of our two private medical units (an infectious disease unit of thirty beds) also closed. There were few private medical patients opting for hospital care except in emergency situations; even cardiac cases avoided hospitalization except in dire need. Anyone with chest or abdominal pain or any other symptoms of serious import thought twice before seeking hospital admission. They felt more secure treating themselves at home, surrounded by the protective presence and loving care of their families.

On July 5, the Obstetric and Gynecology Unit (thirty beds) closed and any patients needing this specialized care were admitted into other units, such as the one private medical unit that continued to function. Every time we had to close a unit, the strain was emotional as well as physical. Patients were transferred to other units, all equipment had to be inventoried and then the doors were chained shut. The heavy chains on one unit door after another were a disturbing visual reminder of our shrinking facilities and no one knew when and if they would ever be removed.

Patients admitted to AUBMC for treatment unrelated to the war came in with great hesitation and fear. To make them feel more secure, we tried to group them together away from the hospital "war scene," but their visitors were constantly exposed in the corridors and elevators to the frightening sight of the armed militia men who insisted on remaining to guard their wounded comrades. Many people preferred to use smaller hospitals in West Beirut or, if they were Christians, cross over to East Beirut for hospital care. Others with the financial means sought medical treatment abroad, in Europe, England or the U.S. Those who had conditions that required special care, such as cardiac cases needing catheterization or emergency surgery, had no other recourse but AUBMC (we had the only coronary care unit in the country). Other admissions included cancer patients undergoing chemotherapy and those with severe complicated symptoms needing a thorough diagnosis. We still had a hard core team of physicians, surgeons and nurses of excellent caliber to handle these cases.

Before the Israeli invasion, the AUBMC nursing staff had numbered 372; a week later it dropped to 182, a loss of 190. The average number of nurses on a unit during a twenty-four-hour period dropped from fourteen to sixteen to eight to three. Here are some of the recorded figures on the sharp decline of staff during that dark summer of 1982:

| Average Number Per Day: | May | July | August | September |
|---|---|---|---|---|
| Patients | 300 | 344 | 350 | 340 |
| Staff Nurses | 225 | 130 | 90 | 126 |
| Practical Nurses | 119 | 51 | 23 | 65 |
| Volunteer Auxiliaries | 183 | 66 | 25 | 78 |
| Floor Clerks | 61 | 26 | 19 | 40 |

It was a case of survival with almost no manpower. How could the nurses and doctors still left cope with such a load? The casualties admitted were very critical: severe blast and shrapnel wounds, burns, life-threatening head and spine injuries. Many had to be placed on respirators and required close attention.

Here is what a typical day in the life of an AUBMC nurse was like during those months. She (the hospital had no male nurses) would be in charge of a thirty-bed unit, let's say, but would have only one nursing assistant and, if she were lucky, the help of a male orderly. She would arrive at work—to an eight-hour shift that often stretched out to sixteen hours—already traumatized and stressed out with worry about her family, often suffering from lack of sleep because of the air raids and shelling. She would start her shift making rounds, from bed to bed, responding to patients shouting for sedation, comforting the pain and tears of children, and checking charts and medical equipment. Then she had to cope with the total dependence of the paraplegics and quadriplegics— who knew they would never walk or move their hands—and with those who were severely burned, who screamed in excruciating pain and needed to be tub-bathed.

In July, a rehabilitation team organized by Dr. Larry Afifi, a nursing instructor, and the wife of an AUBMC physician, removed a heavy load from the nurses' shoulders. Performing functions for the patients that the nursing staff had no time to handle, they went around adjusting pillows and sheets and changing the patients' positions in bed, assisting them in a range of motion exercises, teaching them deep breathing and coughing exercises, and educating both patients and family on attending to a variety of needs that could help ease pain and bring comfort and reassurance.

Once again, foreign volunteer nurses joined the staff— eleven of them this time, recruited from the U.S. and England through the efforts of the Middle East Council of Churches. We also still had around sixty-two Philippine nurses left out of 120 who had originally signed on, but not for long. By July, their number fell to twenty-three, when more than half of them panicked and fled to the safety of East Beirut, where there was no fear of Israeli air raids. There, life was safe and calm, even pleasurable, with people crowding the beaches and partying as if there were no war at all.

We met with the Philippine nurses who remained and were able to convince them to stay, emphasizing that AUBMC was the safest place of all. It was also explained to them that they had no instructions from their consulate to leave West Beirut and that if they crossed over to East Beirut, no authority would be responsible for their safety. We were enormously gratified by the response of those women who, out of their deep sense of commitment, remained at their posts and gave of themselves so willingly.

In August, the Makassed Hospital sent us some of its nursing staff. It had been forced to downsize, because the area in which it was located was under constant bombardment. Under these circumstances, most of the war casualties—the largest number, in fact—ended up at AUBMC.

Munthir Kuzayli, director of the hospital at the time, gave me the responsibility of housing all nurses and other staff and faculty who could not reach home or chose to remain on the AUB campus. Some stayed because they felt needed. Others, whose neighborhoods had become too dangerous, brought their families to live with them in safety at AUB. I will never forget the day in June when Israeli helicopters dropped pink leaflets over West Beirut warning all those still there to leave, or else bear the consequence, and also instructing them to go to East Beirut and towards northern Lebanon via an area where Israeli troops were stationed.

You can imagine the panic that ensued. Everyone took the warning seriously; the Israelis, after all, had shown what damage they could inflict. Everyone was frightened and confused—the hospital staff, patients and visitors—not knowing where to go or what to do. We could not believe the hospital would be hit; the Israelis could not be that inhuman. We felt sure that the big red cross painted on both the roof of the hospital and that of Building 56 would protect us. Nevertheless, we formulated a disaster plan, just in case, and started outlining evacuation procedures. But in no way did this alleviate the wave of chaos that had engulfed the hospital. Everyone wanted to get home to their families and, if God willed it, to die with them. As for me, I had already made the conscious decision to remain whatever the consequences, but how difficult it was to convince those around me to stay. How could I tell a nurse not to worry, that everything would be all right, that we desperately needed her to stay, when all she could think of was getting back to her family? Somehow or other, however, things gradually calmed down and, when I started counting heads, it was a relief to know that most of the staff was still there. I will never forget the terror of those pink leaflets; I still have one to this day.

Day by day, the number of casualties brought into AUBMC increased. On June 11, 174 war-wounded were admitted and by June 23, the number had risen to 193. The terrible sight of the burn cases is still vivid in my memory. Victims of phosphorous bombs, they would arrive in the Emergency Unit literally on fire. Only saline could put out the fire. Their skin was black and puffy, the smell of burning flesh so sickening, their agonized cries of pain so heart-wrenching. There were mothers brought in clasping children in their arms, their hands inseparably welded to each other's bodies. How can man be so inhuman as to create and use such weapons of torturous death?

Burn victims are the most difficult to treat. Simply removing their clothes is so painful that even morphine fails to provide relief. I remember the baby boy that was brought in by a stranger in a box, burnt black and hardly making a whimper. He had no one and could not be identified. Because of the burns, I could not cuddle and comfort him; all I could do was stand by and watch him die. His mother and father were never found and he was listed in the morgue as unknown. To this day, I remember that agonizing sight, that small bundle of burnt flesh. I remember my thoughts, the questions that filled my mind as I looked down at him. Was his mother also dead? What was his name and how old was he? Did he have older brothers and sisters who were still looking for him?

ان جيش الدفاع الاسرائيلي يواصل حربه ضد الخرّبين ولم يستعمل بعد بكامل

قوته انما ليس هو معني بالمس بالمواطنين الابرياء وبمن لم يحارب ضده .

انت الساكن في بيروت .

استغل رقف اطلاق النار وانقذ حياتك .

امامك الامكانيات التالية .

أ . عن طريق قوات جيش الدفاع الاسرائيلي شرقا على محور بيروت — دمشق .

ب . شمالا الى اتجاه طرابلس .

انقذ حياتك وحياة اعزائك .

The terrifying Israeli pink flyer warning Beirut residents to leave the city

In a flood of emotional vulnerability, I broke down into tears, telling myself that if only he had lived I would have adopted and raised him as my own. A nurse came to me and said, "Miss Mouro, why are you crying? Don't worry, with his terrible burns he would have suffered so much if he had lived." Here I was, being consoled by my nurse instead of consoling and providing moral support as I was expected to. I immediately saw that I had to get my emotions back under control. The dead were gone and the living needed every ounce of attention I could give them.

There was not enough space to accommodate all the burn casualties so we had to open the Outpatient Unit and put them there in the corridor. Our available medical and nursing services were stretched to the limit. As for our water supply, there was hardly enough to cover drinking and cooking needs, let alone filling an entire tub of water to soak a

The aftermath of an Israeli air raid: bodies in the rubble

burn patient in. (Hot water, need I add, had become a distant memory by then.) It took ingenuity to gather the water needed for the patient tub baths, storing every drop we could find in a large container. Burn patients were bathed only once every 24 hours. We had only one tub to work with, which meant that tub bathing went on all day—and with it the shouting and screaming, especially from the children, whose piercing cries reverberated throughout the hospital.

As the days went by, it was rewarding to see a patient recover and begin the series of operations that would graft new skin over the burn-scarred areas. I especially remember Nisrine, the six-year-old who spent two and a half years with us until all the operations were completed. She, of course, became the hospital "pet."

Of the many casualties that poured into the AUBMC Emergency Unit, about ten percent were dead on arrival, twenty-five percent were admitted and the remaining sixty-five percent not requiring hospitalization were given stop-gap treatment on the spot. Several clinics and small medical centers opened in Beirut to handle those with minor injuries. The Near East School of Theology, for instance, was turned into a hospital run by Palestinians and a group of foreign medical professionals. I visited the center one day and was amazed by its facilities and organization. They had created a good-sized, efficient underground hospital, very secure and safe from shelling; they could rely on the Red Crescent (the Muslim Red Cross) for a steady provision of the medical supplies they needed; and the Dutch, Swedish and German doctors and nurses working there were committed, top-notch professionals.

During the short hours spent away from the hospital, we tried to give some measure of normalcy to our lives. On the half-day off of my seven-day work week, I would go jogging on the AUB campus, up and down its beautiful seaside slopes and around its soccer field. I would run and run, ignoring the danger of stray bullets. I did not care. It kept me sane.

The few friends that remained, however, became one of the most important elements in keeping us all grounded. Spending our days together, sharing our joys and sorrows, helping each other out of depressions, we depended on each other and became very close. It's curious how one can adapt to some things and not to others. As food became scarcer in besieged Beirut, we got used to a dreary, limited diet. But there were two "delicacies" that I personally could not give up—crackers and Coffee-Mate. Whenever anyone was going outside Beirut, I would ask them to bring me back a box of crackers and a jar of Coffee-Mate.

On July 3, an Israeli blockade was enforced on West Beirut and for ninety days we were cut off from fruits and vegetables and many other fresh foods. There was hardly enough food for the patients, never mind the staff, volunteers, visitors and others, and we had to follow a strict schedule of food rationing. Our meals became rice and beans and beans and rice day after day, seven days a week.

On top of this, there was not enough gas or oil to feed the University's central power plant, the only source of electricity and steam for the AUB campus and hospital. Its fuel consumption was cut from 20,000 liters a day to 7,000, and we had to take strong measures to conserve energy. Oxygen usage also had to be reduced and carefully rationed to the most needy patients. And we began running low on medical supplies, even though the hospital usually had a six-month stockpile of all essentials.

One evening, when the staff from the Dean's office moved into our offices on the first floor of the hospital and were sleeping there because of the heavy shelling, I managed to get a bag of apples I had found in storage in the kitchen. I still remember how their faces lit up with surprised joy, like children getting toys at Christmas.

The celebration of my birthday on August 2 is a typical example of the depths of deprivation we experienced that summer. But to this day, it remains one of my fondest memories. In preparing the surprise party they gave me, my friends had to improvise all the way. There was no shop around selling birthday cards, so they made me one out of colored electrocardiographic labels. There was no bakery open, but they managed to find one piece of cake in a nearby restaurant and placed a candle on it (as our substitute for electricity, we had plenty of candles). As for the birthday dinner, it turned out to be the five of us sharing a bowl of tuna salad, garnished by one cut-up tomato from the garden of the University's Department of Agriculture. But surprise of surprises, my friends came up

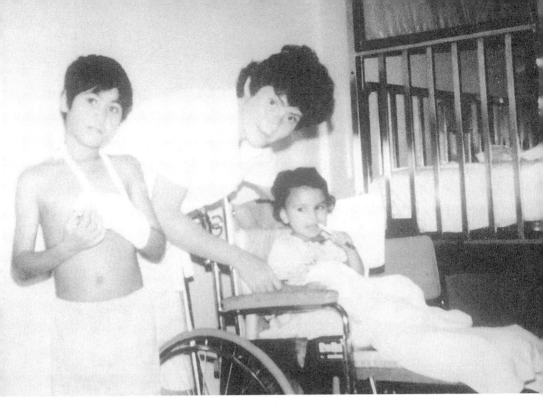

With Nisrine and another patient in the pediatric ward

with a bottle of perfume as my birthday gift.

Interludes like this, when human goodness and fellow-ship graced our lives, made all the difference. Most of the time, the nurses were depressed, anxious and exhausted, faced every minute of the day by the double challenge of fulfilling their responsibility to others and concern for their own survival. The doctors were not always on hand—busy either in the operating rooms or in the Emergency Unit—and it was the nurse who had to deal with all the human repercussions of sudden bombardment and moving patients into corridors or positioning their beds away from windows and flying shrapnel.

The nurse was on the front line, dealing with many help-less individuals—from critical patients to those who were ambulatory but would suddenly go into shock or panic and become hysterical. Every minute and action counted and a

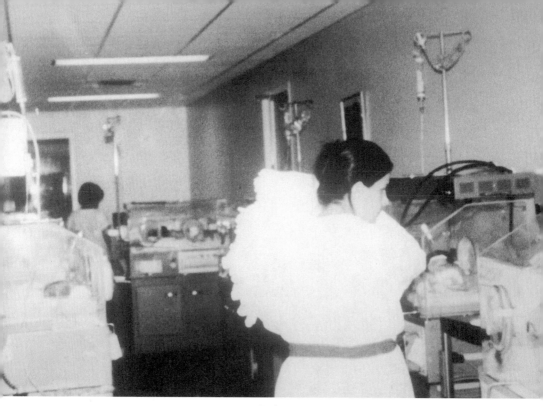

Work at AUBMC continues in the safety of the corridors

small mistake could be fatal. The guiding dictum was never to lose control, always to work calmly and efficiently.

During the invasion, the rooms on the top tenth floor of the hospital overlooked an area that was a constant air raid target, which meant that the upper floors—from the eighth on up—were more dangerous than the lower floors. Therefore, every time there was an air raid, we had to move the top floor patients down to the basement where they would be safe. In ironic contrast, because of the ground-to-ground missile shelling that went on during the civil conflict between East and West Beirut, it was the lower floors that were more dangerous.

During bombardments, the hospital nursery, with a total of fifty babies, needed the most attention. Totally helpless creatures born into a world of pain, their lives depended on our presence and help. It was the first area I ran to when the bombs started falling, to help in moving the babies to safer quarters. On the adult units, visitors helped move patients, but sometimes they proved to be a liability, adding to the chaos with their screaming and panicked reactions. Patients in traction were difficult to move, as were those on respirators. And because we did not have enough beds in the Intensive Care Unit, critically ill patients were scattered throughout the hospital.

Patients were transported to the basement one by one, with identifying nametags on their beds. Medication lists, ECG machines, defibrillators, infusions and all other needed supplies and equipment also had to be moved and marked with the patient's name. Everyone had to be very careful not to make mistakes, not to mix one patient with another and in confusion administer the wrong treatment or medication.

A nurse never knew where each patient was until she started passing out medication. If she was on the tenth floor and could not find the patient she was looking for, she would check out the lounge; and if the patient was not there, she would go down to the basement. It was like a game of hide and seek. Sometimes a nurse would yell that she could not find her patient. And instead of Florence Nightingale's lamp, we had to use flashlights when the lights suddenly went off.

Some of the patients refused to go to the basement and insisted on staying where they were. We did not have time to argue with them. Actually, we did not have space in the basement to accommodate all of them. It was my job to double-check on all the patients everywhere, from the top floor on down to the basement. To make sure all patients were accounted for, I had an alphabetized list of patients that I updated daily with the Emergency Unit admitting clerk.

It was a very painful summer for all of us. We felt lost, cut off from family and not knowing when the nightmare would end. Those who left West Beirut to escape the bombardment were later looked upon as deserters when they returned. Some were nurses, who should have remained as we did. They tried to justify their action, saying that they wanted to stay but could not because they were too scared or their families would not let them. This sometimes angered me; I was just as scared as they were, and my family was thousands of miles away.

The resident medical staff that remained numbered around 160, with an attendance rate of seventy-five percent. Elective surgery ceased, the Outpatient Department and Private Clinics were closed and, as expected in such critical situations, pediatric and medical cases decreased. Very few medical emergency cases came in. Either patients treated themselves or went to their own physicians for treatment. Some who were critically ill and left themselves untreated just died at home.

One day, we almost lost the Emergency Unit itself, and with it three of our staff. Armed men rushed in carrying one of their militiamen who had a serious shrapnel injury. He was taken into the x-ray room and placed on the table there. A couple of minutes later, the entire Emergency Unit shook from a thundering explosion. Nurse Sirvart Yegavian, who was at the surgical desk with her floor clerk, wheeled around and was relieved to see the x-ray technician stumbling out of an adjoining room. When the dust settled and the three women looked into the x-ray room, they saw pieces of human flesh splattered against the walls. A hand grenade in the militiaman's trousers had exploded. The x-ray machine was totally destroyed and the room was closed for weeks until the smell of burnt flesh had disappeared.

Emile Jeha, Assistant Director of the Physical Plant, was one of the few who remained to ensure the operation of the hospital and University. He was adept at bargaining with the various militia factions to secure water and with government officials to supply electricity. He even handled dealing with the Israeli Army during its occupation of Beirut in his constant efforts to fill the water and power needs of the hospital. He was remarkable—available at all times with a smile on his face, never refusing any request and always knowing what to do. He knew every single area of the medical center and moved swiftly to repair damage or address problems before a crisis could occur. It would have been almost impossible to keep the hospital functioning without him. To all of us, he exuded a sense of security, a feeling of "Do not worry, all will be well" that was reassuring.

Other parts of the country faced similar challenges. I had a friend who worked as a nurse in the mountains, where shelling and air raids also occurred during the Israeli invasion. As in Beirut, there were hardly any beds left in her small 100-bed hospital. Patients were placed in corridors. Only critical cases were kept at the hospital, while those in stable condition were transferred to nearby hotels, where they were taken care of by volunteers trained in basic nursing care.

An important event entered my life in March 1982. This was my relationship with Nabil, an intern I met at the hospital. We had a piano in our dormitory that he used to practice on every day. A mutual friend introduced us and gradually we became close friends. There was no place to go, so we would walk for hours and hours through the campus, sharing our worries and our dreams. I would tell him about my problems in the hospital and he would tell me about his. He was an extremely bright individual and I enjoyed so much hearing him talk about medicine and his plans for the future. We spent every spare moment together, day after day, evening after evening, when he would often play the piano for me. And as the months passed, I began to wonder about and imagine a future life with Nabil.

In the fall of 1982, I left Lebanon for the U.S. when I received a grant from AUB to pursue a master's degree in nursing at the University of Pennsylvania. I felt privileged and was pleased to go, but I missed the hospital and I missed Nabil. No sooner had I arrived at the University than I began inquiring whether Nabil could be admitted for an elective course. He had top scores and was immediately accepted. We had two wonderful months together; then in December, with the semester almost over, we decided to return to Lebanon together for Christmas. He had finished his course and I had three weeks between semesters and wanted to be with him. The plan was to go to Beirut, talk to his parents and get engaged. I would then finish my degree in the U.S., he would apply there for a residency and we could begin our life together.

It was not meant to be. When Nabil's mother learned about our plans, she objected strongly, telling him I was just a nurse, and an American besides, and insisted that he look for a Lebanese girl to marry, a rich girl with social status that would be an asset to him in his career. When Nabil told me about his mother's reaction, I realized he was torn between his love for me and his love and respect for his mother. He was lost. I was shocked.

I was also furious, and all the love I had for Nabil turned to regret and sadness. Although I knew he wanted to marry me, I also knew how much control his mother had over him. I immediately ended our relationship and I never saw him again. Emotionally, it was an extremely painful period and I became very depressed. But I was determined that I would get over Nabil and I knew that my devotion to nursing would serve as the best antidote for the pain I was feeling.

A man carrying what is left of his house

Chapter Five
# More Fighting, More Fears, More Shortages

I returned to the U.S. in January 1983, completed my degree, but decided not to stay for graduation because I was needed at AUBMC. Once again, when I wanted so much to attend a graduation ceremony and wear a cap and gown, I could not. Although the Israelis had withdrawn from Beirut and the PLO had moved to Tunis, the civil war was still going on in Lebanon. While I was gone, the U.S. Embassy and marine barracks had become targets of deadly car bombs. I wanted to get back as soon as I could.

As I was preparing my travel plans, I received a telephone call from Dr. Raja Khuri, Dean of the AUB Medical School, who was in the U.S. on a brief visit. He asked to meet with me; I could not imagine why and wondered if I had done something wrong. We met in AUB's New York office and, then and there, he asked me if I would assume the position of Director of Nursing Services at AUBMC. I looked at him as though he were talking to the wrong person. He must be mistaken, I thought. I was stunned and stood speechless for a few seconds. He waited for me to answer. Of course, I said yes. But all the while, my mind was reeling with the reality of it: Gladys Mouro, Director of Nursing Services...one of the most important positions in the hospital and so vital to its functioning. Could I handle it? How would I deal with all those twice my age?

I had a long way to go and a lot of learning to do, with few resources or people to provide guidance. Once in Beirut again, I began by reviewing all previous office records and correspondence, reading every office file to understand how the administrative system worked, meeting with people on all levels and in the various departments of the hospital. I realized I had two strikes against me: I was young and inexperienced and the hospital was in a war zone. The challenge, however, excited me and gradually I developed my own management techniques and style.

I remember the first time I held a meeting of head nurses. So many of them were twice my age and I had to instill in them a feeling of trust and confidence in me. People always imagine nursing directors as old, tough-looking, know-it-all characters. I did not fit that image. I was young, not yet thirty, an attractive blond, and inexperienced. I was also an American at a time when U.S. policy was not popular in Lebanon. I had to prove to my nurses, to my senior staff, to the doctors, to all of AUBMC, and even to the militias, that I could cope with the responsibility. Most of all, I had to prove it to myself. I was proud to be a nurse and it meant everything to me to become one of the best. I would be leading a nursing staff of 677 people, effecting change and making decisions that could sometimes involve the risk of error. It would not be easy, but I was determined to succeed.

We thought that with the Israelis and the PLO gone,

peace would now prevail in Lebanon. We did not know we would be experiencing another decade of war, another kind of internal conflict waged for different reasons and by different political factions. No sooner did we find out which militia controlled our area and who its leader was, than another group would take over. With each change, we became the unwilling captive audience of a whole new play made up of different actors (militiamen), a different director (militia leader) and a different script (battle plan). And each time, the hospital staff was there, healing fighters who would return once more to the battle. We saw no finale to this play; it went on and on and on.

If I had to choose the worst emotion, it would be fear. Fear remains the most unbearable and stressful emotion a human being can experience, and it often leaves wounds too deep to heal. As Franklin Delano Roosevelt once said, "The only thing we have to fear is fear itself." I wonder if I would have stayed on had I known in 1982 that another eight years of war and fear were still ahead of me.

In a symposium of psychologists, psychiatrists and sociologists held at AUB in 1983, one of the speakers commented,

> *People are remarkably able to adjust to incredible circumstances. Water, electricity and food were cut off, there was constant shelling, and somehow or other, these people maintained their psychological integrity. But what we're afraid of is: what happens when people can let go, when the stress is lifted and people can relax? They have not been able to do this yet. The question is what will happen when they do?*

The full psychological impact of war would not be felt until peace was restored.

At the beginning of 1983, the effects of the preceding eight years of violence on the mental health of the Lebanese were only partially apparent. In an article by Lydia Georgi in a March issue of the Beirut weekly *Monday Morning*, AUB Professor Nadim Khalaf was quoted as saying:

> *The Lebanese society is in a state of anomie,*
> *people have become victims of a chronic condition*
> *of seeking without fulfillment. Demoralization*
> *has become so endemic that foul and illegitimate*
> *means have become necessary to attain desired*
> *goals. The war has aggravated decadence in*
> *public life. The Lebanese have been exposed to*
> *the terror and brutality which accompany naked*
> *violence and civil unrest. They have been tutored*
> *and socialized into violence. Human aggression*
> *has been transformed into an innate desire for*
> *destructiveness or a compulsion to kill. The*
> *way people have resorted or coped with this*
> *demoralization is through a general mood of*
> *indifference and entropy. Yet this accumulation*
> *of discontent, pent-up resentment and impotent*
> *hostility is bound to manifest itself in symptoms*
> *of psychic distress and personality disorders.*

A leading Lebanese psychiatrist, Dr. Antranic Manougian, who was director of the Asfourieh Hospital for Mental and Nervous Disorders that closed during the war, observed that people generally tend to be healthier mentally during stressful situations than after the stressful situation has ended. This has been our experience at AUBMC. In 1994 we had at least four admissions per day of mentally and emotionally disturbed patients, and today we are still treating many patients suffering from the psychological effects of the war. To fill the continuing need AUBMC is now in the process of establishing a full-scale psychiatric unit. Dar Al Saleeb, a 1000-bed institution that is Lebanon's primary psychiatric hospital, can hardly keep up with the demand for in-patient care.

The 1983 casualty figures went up and down according to whether the political climate was stormy or calm. Conditions of security were somewhat better than the year before, but no one was optimistic about the future. Did I have the energy to go on? I was very tired and although I knew I could leave if I wished, I just could not make that decision. I felt that as long as I was needed, I had to stay.

Running a wartime hospital calls for special modifications in the organization of facilities. In the Emergency Unit, we set up an overnight ward with two trolleys equipped with the supplies needed for mass casualties, including surgical kits and linen, so that treatment could be started immediately. In addition, we had eight tables that could be used as stretchers if none were available. We continually evaluated our staff in terms of function, distribution and chain of command. We reviewed the functions of the housekeeper, the central sterilizing worker, the telephone operator, the morgue technician, the pharmacist, the security guard and all other hospital employees, so that each knew specifically what he or she should do in case of a disaster.

Our contingency plan was revised and a new disaster team was formed. Any rush of thirty or more casualties into the Emergency Unit would be considered a disaster. The nurse in charge, in coordination with the surgical resident, would call the Emergency Unit director, the hospital director, the nursing director and the chief of staff and declare a disaster. All members of the house staff would then be paged to proceed immediately to the Emergency Unit.

Triaging—the sorting out and assigning of casualties

according to treatment priority—was extremely important, not only to assure that critical cases received
immediate care, but also to avoid disorganization. The
surgical resident or the nurse supervisor would assign
patients to specific cubicles, and those with major injuries
were sent to pre-op surgery rooms and from there to the
operating suites. Very often, however, armed militiamen
interfered with the triage process. They would take over the
Emergency Unit as though it were their own property, each
group insisting that their wounded be taken care of first
and threatening the doctors and nurses if they refused.

The casualties were mostly brought in by trucks or
armed jeeps, accompanied by friends who improvised
emergency sirens by firing their automatic high-powered
rifles in the air. Often the injured were without
identification other than what they could orally furnish.
Then began the tense and vital work of sorting the patients.
Those who were conscious shouted for attention and often
their accompanying comrades would threaten the staff with
guns or grenades. Once, when a doctor slapped a patient in
shock in an effort to revive him, the patient's friend took
offense and starting shooting off his machine gun in the air.
Everyone ducked and the poor doctor ran out and up five
flights of stairs with the gunman chasing him and, not far
behind, his militia friends who were finally able to stop him.

One of the Emergency Unit supervisors, Rosine
Yeralian, who daily experienced confrontations with gunmen, had a special knack in calming them down. She was
a loving personality who always spoke to the militiamen
in a soothing way, saying "*Habibi* (sweetheart), take it
easy, do not worry, we will take care of everything." It was
remarkable people like her who very often made the
difference in dangerous situations.

The Emergency Unit contained three major surgery

rooms and five minor surgery cubicles, plus medical and pediatric wings that were used when the surgical areas were full, which was often. When mass casualties came in, complete chaos would prevail for five to ten minutes, with patients screaming, hospital staff shouting, and blood spurting everywhere. Patients would be placed on benches, on the floor, anywhere, and immediate treatment would be initiated. This was when we would get the trolleys out and open the emergency overnight ward. Within ten minutes, all the patients had been triaged and placed in the proper treatment unit. Depending on the extent of their injuries, they were either given immediate treatment and sent home or admitted for surgery. We had continuous problems with the availability of beds, especially at night when other hospitals closed their doors

The Emergency Room closes due to a strike provoked by the kidnapping of the hospital director and the comptroller

and all cases were diverted to AUBMC. At such times, because of our reduced staff and limited supplies, we also had to apply the triaging process to hospital admissions— only critical non-transferable cases were admitted, among them those with serious intracranial injuries requiring surgery that could not be performed at any other hospital.

It was also at such times that the experience and skills of the nurse supervisor were most essential. She had to ensure there were enough supplies, linen and staff. She had to find or improvise beds and see that the surgery and recovery units were prepared to receive patients. She also had to take care of the dead, to make sure they were all properly identified, and if lacking identification, labeled as unknown.

It was the supervisor who had to be there while the pockets or purses of the dead were emptied of valuables and money to make sure nothing was stolen. Many would arrive at the hospital with large sums of money (up to the equivalent of thousands of dollars sometimes). Throughout the war, because most banks were closed, people carried their money with them. At first, I had great difficulty in performing this ghastly function, especially when the body was gouged and dismembered, when before me lay intestines spilling out, severed limbs or a gaping hole where the face had been. To make matters worse, bystanders would crowd in and silently watch what was going on—strongly reminding me of a "vultures of death" scenario in a Greek tragedy.

The Emergency Unit bore the brunt of all the crises caused by the dangerous behavior of the militias, who were a law unto themselves. In a "normal" war, a hospital is expected to serve only one side or the other, never both; at AUBMC, we were caught in a treacherous middle, trying to serve both sides (or several opposing sides) equally and still cope with the threats that rained upon us.

One evening, when two opposing factions brought their wounded in to the Emergency Unit at the same time, the gunmen of one militia warned the hospital staff to ignore one of the patients because he was their enemy. The patient was dying and we, in turn, ignored the threats and took care of him. At one stage, to prevent armed men from driving down the street between the Emergency Unit and the hospital, shooting their guns in the air to sound an alarm, large blocks of cement were positioned at the upper entrance of the hospital to serve as a checkpoint.

In crossing the street from the hospital to the Emergency Unit, I always ducked down and ran across to dodge stray bullets. I also kept a sharp eye out for the speeding jeeps or vans loaded with wounded that would suddenly appear from nowhere and come to a screeching halt at the emergency doors. A pedestrian's safety, even though that pedestrian was a nurse who could save their lives, meant nothing to them.

Those responsible for the hospital's security could do nothing. They were no match for these armed-to-the-teeth, freewheeling warriors. Some of us tried to calm them down, but to no avail. Many of these men came in drugged and had no control over their actions. This is what scared us most. Our only prayer was that no one would be shot accidentally. One militiaman who demanded immediate attention grabbed a hand grenade and waved it at us, threatening to throw it. We all hit the floor and scurried under whatever cover we could find. Fortunately, one of the saner militia characters, obviously with leadership status, stepped in and defused the situation.

Each militia group had its own health representatives in the hospital, who were always there monitoring the care of their fighters. They knew all the ins and outs of the hospital, how to get a patient admitted, what papers to pre-pare, which physicians to contact, where to get supplies, everything. The press people of each militia also were always there, demanding lists of the dead or wounded.

There was not a single staff member at AUBMC that did not at one time or another experience terrifying moments. One day, several fighters burst into the Emergency Unit, shouting and shooting, pushing through one cubicle after another, apparently looking for one specific patient. Then they suddenly started fighting with each other, one group against the other, which threw everyone around into panicked flight. In the pediatric unit, mothers grabbed their children and ran. In the medical section, a cardiac patient developed cardiac arrest and died on the spot. Other patients and staff hid out in the bathroom. One of the fighters, wielding the hand grenade threat, forced an intern to give him his lab coat—he wanted to disguise himself as a doctor to more easily find the man he was looking for. He did find him and promptly shot him dead. Five men were wounded in that day's shooting, and for the next week the Emergency Unit remained closed to repair the damage.

From time to time, a wave of Lebanese roulette would sweep the capital, when many innocent people became the targets of stray bullets or sniper fire. The snipers would hide on the upper floors of buildings, peer out the window and take aim at anyone that crossed their path, not asking or caring who the target was.

During both the civil war and the Israeli invasion, the operating room staff functioned with extraordinary capability. Moving without stop from one surgical case to another, they managed to cope with shortages of personnel and supplies. Some patients were brought into the operating suite still in their bloody clothes, with little time to follow proper surgical procedures. Sometimes gunmen would push in by force to watch and ensure that the operation was actually being performed.

Dr. Anis Baraka, Chairman of the Anesthesia Department, wrote the following in an article that appeared in the *Middle East Journal of Anesthesiology* (1983) about the major obstacle his department faced:

*We were short of everything, but the most important shortage was that of oxygen and nitrous oxide supply. We started to economize gas by using low flows of oxygen and nitrous oxide via a carbon dioxide absorption circuit. We put all respirators that were driven by oxygen (OHIO, BIRD) out of circulation. When we became completely short of oxygen and nitrous oxide, we used compressors to feed room air into anesthesia machines, but it was very noisy and we had to stop their use and depend on simple drawover techniques.*

The operating room staff was always on call from the Emergency Unit to prepare for operations as needed. AUBMC had a total of ten operating suites, but from time to time some would close because of shortage of staff. I remember one night when twenty-three major operations were performed within eight hours and when one single surgeon performed thirteen craniotomies within a period of thirty-six hours. The youngest casualty was not even born: a woman in her eighth month of pregnancy had been shot and the bullet had lodged in the head of the fetus. The second youngest was eleven days old, an infant who was injured at home by flying shrapnel from a nearby rocket blast. Most casualties brought into the operating room were between fifteen and thirty years of age. A twenty-five-year-old pregnant woman on her way to the hospital to deliver sustained shrapnel injuries to her eyes, neck, torso and limbs. She underwent an emergency laparotomy (the surgical opening of the abdomen) and a stillbirth was delivered followed by a right thoracotomy (surgical incision of the chest wall) and exploration of the neck. Usually, patients with chest injuries and cardiac tamponade (compression) received the highest priority in the operating room, followed by those with injuries to the head and to large blood vessels.

To avoid potential conflict in staff responsibilities, one individual was chosen to establish and implement priorities. Throughout the day and night, there was always a senior nurse in charge of the operating room to coordinate the on-call staff and initiate preparations for surgery. At all times, an emergency team was present in the operating room, which was also supported by the recovery unit nursing staff. Each member of each team

A French soldier helps a casualty of US Embassy bombing

knew exactly what to do. It was important not only to establish and treat the physical condition of the patient, but also to respond to his or her emotional needs. They were unprepared and frightened, and the comfort of a soft touch and sympathetic words were essential, explaining what was happening and why, respecting their dignity and reassuring them of our protection and care.

The operating room nursing staff faced the constant problem of a casualty being rushed in for surgery with militiamen following right behind. The only way they were stopped from entering the operating room was to impress upon them the fact that they would contaminate the room and thus endanger the patient's life. They were also told that the doors had to be kept open because of the excessive heat in the room and the heavy perspiration of the staff, due to no air conditioning, which increased the risk of infection. Once the false ceiling in one of the operating suites fell because of leaking pipes caused by a rocket that had hit the fourth floor. Staff members were kept busy for two hours collecting water to prevent it from reaching sterile supplies. Male physicians often had to wear scrub dresses, especially when the water supply was cut off and all available scrub suits piled up in the non-functioning laundry.

Like all other units in the hospital, the operating room had its contingency plan. If there were more casualties than the night team could handle, the evening team would stay on to help. In case of mass casualties, all operating room nurses living in the hospital or on campus were called in. In extreme situations, all operating room nurses living near the hospital were contacted and a car was made available to transport them to the hospital.

Towards the end of 1983, staff absenteeism increased to seventy percent. It was an extremely difficult period, marked by an increased workload and a general feeling of insecurity.

## Chapter Six

# AUB's Tragic Loss

On January 18, 1984, Malcolm Kerr, the president of AUB, was assassinated. Two gunmen had casually taken the unguarded elevator to the third floor in College Hall, swept swiftly down the corridor, past the startled secretary and into the president's office. They shot him, seated at his desk, then quickly escaped before anyone knew what was happening. While Dr. Kerr was being taken to Emergency, I received a call from the Dean's office to get to the unit immediately. There, I found doctors and nurses desperately working to keep him alive, but it was no use. His long, lean body lay flat on the stretcher, blood pouring out of his head. He was 52-years-old, so young and athletic in body. It was an unbelievable tragedy.

Dr. Kerr's wife, Ann, had come to the Emergency Unit when she heard her husband had been shot. She now had to be told that her husband was dead. Dr. Khuri asked me to be with her when he gave her the terrible news. As I embraced her, she cried softly like a child in bewildered

The aftermath of
a car bombing

pain and kept repeating, "Why? Why? Why?" Once again, as with Dean Najemy's wife, I was at a loss to know what to say, how to comfort her, other than to hold her close and let my arms convey whatever comfort they could. Ann Kerr showed remarkable courage through it all, handling all she had to endure with great dignity. The first thing she did when we accompanied her to Marquand House, the president's residence on campus, was to enter the privacy of her bedroom to telephone their four children in the U.S. and, with each anguished call, relate the stark reality of the tremendous grief that now engulfed the Kerr family.

Dr. Kerr's assassination, recognized as the direct result of America's military presence in Lebanon along with its continuing pro-Israeli policies, marked the beginning of threats to foreigners. On the same day, the Saudi Arabian consul was kidnapped. Ironically, Dr. Kerr had predicted in one of his talks that 1984 would be the most difficult year since 1976 for AUB.

President Kerr became the innocent victim of that explosive atmosphere. He had arrived in Beirut in September 1982 to take over the presidency after David Dodge, acting president at the time, was kidnapped (then released a year later). His sole objective was to keep AUB open and functioning. He not only kept the University open, but also gave it a renewed sense of purpose and vitality. He was admired and respected by all. His ashes were buried on the AUB campus, on the playground of his youth and in the country where he was born.

Beirut's *Daily Star* wrote:

*The irony about Dr. Kerr is that he had a long record of writing and research in support of the Arabs. He was born at the American University of*

*Beirut Medical Center in 1931. His father Stanley
Kerr taught medicine at AUB and his mother
served as Dean of Woman Students. He received his
Bachelor's degree at Princeton University in 1953,
then returned to AUB, where he received his
Master's degree. His thesis and first book was titled
Lebanon in the Last Years of Feudalism: 1840-1868.
Why was this honorable and valuable human being
killed? Was it an act against the U.S.? Was it to
destroy the institutional and academic strength
of AUB? No one really knows.*

In February, fighting again flared up among the different political groups, back and forth between East and West Beirut. Seventeen shells hit the University campus and students had to evacuate the Basic Sciences Building, which had served as a shelter since the beginning of the war. Students were granted a period of guided study and optional examinations to end in March, and a provisional date was set for the start of the second semester.

At the hospital, we again began to face shortages. We were very low on supplies and oxygen and were down to only a two-week supply of fuel and gas. Oxygen had to be administered selectively. It came from the east, and special arrangements had to be made with the militias in control to allow it to be transported across the front lines of battle—often for a price. But the stock of food still in storage at least assured us of meals—enough to feed as many as 3,000 people on some days. Housing, however, once more presented problems. Everyone who came to the hospital wanted to stay there.

February was a dreadful month. All ten operating suites were functioning full-time. The working hours of nurses jumped to 2,000 hours of overtime per month for a staff of fifty. Under-staffing became so serious that a public plea was made in the press to all employees, urging them to return to work and assuring them of protective transportation from their homes.

One night, I stayed in the hospital until four o'clock in the morning. All the militias that had staked out their own territories in West Beirut were shooting at each other. It was as though a volcano had erupted and I was sure the Emergency Unit would get its share. For the first few hours, we received no casualties—the intensity of fighting had prevented the Red Cross from transporting the wounded. Then suddenly, they began pouring in—some civilians, but mostly fighters from the different militias, some dead, some alive, and with them came their angry armed comrades. We were all scared they would start shooting at each other and we would be caught in the middle. One of the militiamen looked at me while I was delegating nursing duties and, suspecting I was an American, asked me who I was. He shouted at me that I was not welcome, that I should leave, that the war was all America's fault and that no American should be allowed to remain in Lebanon. It was not pleasant, and so very ironic, to hear this after all I had been going through to save the lives of his comrades. Fortunately, the head of Lebanese Army Security was able to calm him down. At that point, I was tired and wanted to go home. I was not living on campus at the time, but in a staff apartment nearby. I knew it was risky to leave the hospital, but I needed to get away for a few hours and sleep in my own bed instead of in my office.

Then there was the day when about 150 casualties were rushed in after a bomb exploded in a cinema. The situation was more or less stable at the time and people had begun going to the movies again. The scene in the emergency room was similar to what I had experienced when I was a student nurse—only this time I was a supervisor and responsible for the organization that was so essential in times of crisis. That night, as I did on so many other nights, I lay awake reliving the day's experience. I remembered the handsome young boy with green eyes and black hair, lying on the floor, his eyes pleading for help. I remember standing by him when he closed his eyes and died. I remember my sorrow, my feelings of helplessness and the blind anger that flooded my being at the cruelty and madness of a conflict that victimized so many innocents.

As the days went by, things got worse. Many stray bullets found their way into patients' rooms. It was always random, never confined to one specific wing or floor, so

The carnage continues: retrieving the dead and injured from the rubble

it made no sense to vacate rooms. We had bullets on all the upper floors, from the sixth to the tenth, in pediatrics, obstetrics, medicine and surgery. One of our Philippine nurses on the tenth floor was wounded while administering medication to a patient. Fortunately for the patient, she was standing between him and the window and caught the bullet instead. We positioned the beds away from the windows as best we could. Some patients refused to stay in their rooms and moved into the corridors and lounge; others refused to leave their rooms regardless of the danger. And when the shelling got heavy, we did not know where to move them. The basement was not big enough and inconveniently too far away from the upper floors.

Housing was also a problem during this critical time. With the hospital transportation services at a standstill, many staff members lived at AUB and some brought their families with them. We had to accommodate them all. We were able to house the women in Building 56, but it was difficult to find accommodations for the men. Some slept in patients' rooms, in kitchens, on stretchers, on the floor or in bathtubs. We were running out of towels and sheets and barely had enough left for the patients. The Dietary Department also began running out of food. Patients and staff had to be fed, and it was not easy to bring in food supplies under gunfire, which meant that we went back once again to the only meal that could feed so many hungry people—rice and beans.

The militiamen coming to visit their wounded—and often to sleep in their rooms—were difficult to control. They would force their way into the hospital, waving their weapons and acting as if they owned the hospital. No one could stop them; they were at the peak of their power and we had no choice but to take it or leave it. More than anything else, it was this situation that caused so many staff, doctors and key personnel to leave.

The University itself was passing through a double-edged crisis—no leadership and no money—and the struggle to retain or recruit top-quality faculty and maintain its high academic standards became increasingly difficult. The politicians and militias could not care less. The murder of the president may have been no more than a blind act of anti-American hatred, but it robbed us of a true leader and scholar. The consensus among AUB's senior administrators was that it was essential for the University to maintain its American connection and preserve the American system of education it embodied. But it was almost impossible to replace Dr. Kerr with another American president. The University kept falling under the control of one political faction after another. Before the Israelis entered West Beirut in 1982, Palestinian and leftist Arab nationalist groups had been the dominant political force on campus. After the election of Amin Gemayel as president of Lebanon, the Lebanese Army tried to establish control, but they were soon pushed aside by the militias of the PSP (the mostly Druze Progressive Socialist Party) and Amal (mostly Shiites), who in February 1984 took over West Beirut as the dominating powers. They often tried to pressure those of us in senior positions and, seeking more power, tried to take over key positions at AUB. It became harder and harder for the University to maintain objectivity in its educational standards and in the appointment of faculty at the University, but many risked their lives to do so. In the hospital, our fear was that political control would influence staff appointments or admissions and, in consequence, would certainly drive away more personnel.

An off-campus extension of AUB, which had opened in

1977 in the East, continued to operate for those students who could not safely travel to West Beirut. Although the inhabitants of West Beirut were a mixture of Christians and Moslems, many Christians of East Beirut were afraid to cross over into "enemy territory." The rumors that the University might move out of West Beirut entirely began circulating, but they were groundless. It was clear that AUB would remain on the campus where it was founded. Many of the faculty had left in 1976, followed by more departures during the Israeli invasion, but many loyalists remained.

In the hospital, the flight of doctors, and more frequently of nurses, continued. They were no longer able to cope with the ugly, frightening situation. The militiamen had become increasingly difficult to handle. Often drugged, with many of them hard-core addicts, they were no longer rational. Some, manifesting signs of drug withdrawal, would yell at the nurses for sedation and throw anything they could get their hands on. Once, when I was making rounds with one of the nurses, one of the patients who had been in the hospital for almost three months, demanded an injection of Demerol. When we told him he had just received a shot and was not scheduled another, he hurled his food tray at us and swiftly pulled out a pistol from under his pillow. Fortunately, his friends jumped on him and took the gun away. For a moment, I thought my life was over.

Armed men roaming the halls were another kind of danger. One day, soon after a fighter was admitted to 8 South in critical condition, militiamen from a rival faction—who were roving the halls and evidently saw him brought in—showed up with guns. They demanded that 8 North, which was closed due to lack of staff, be opened and that they be allowed to move the patient there "to guard" him. They threatened the evening supervisor, who left supposedly to get the key, but instead ran to another unit to call for help. She was sure they wanted to kill him. The next day the patient was no longer there. We heard he had died and was taken to the morgue during the night. Nobody knew or was willing to admit how it happened.

Families sometimes gave us cause to worry, too. Once, a patient on a respirator, a paraplegic with a bullet in his spine, suffered a cardiac arrest and died while the nurses were making their morning rounds. The family reacted with fury, cursing the nurses as though they had caused their son's death. Another incident that ended more happily occurred between two casualties sharing the same room. Both were intubated, on respirators, and conscious. (We had no surgical intensive care area and those patients on respirators were distributed in various units throughout the hospital.) During the night, one of the men noticed that the other's respirator tube was disconnected and that no alarm had gone off. He kept ringing his bell and making all sorts of noises until a nurse heard him and rushed in to reconnect the respirator. Imagine a patient, helpless, unable to move or breathe on his own, saving his roommate's life!

Cooking in the patients' rooms became common- place. In spite of the smoke and smell, families fried pota- toes and eggplant. They boiled the head and legs of lamb in our metal flower vases to prepare nourishing broth, believing that bone gelatin was the best cure for their wounded. They chopped parsley, mint, tomatoes and onion on our bedside tables to make *tabbouleh*, the pop- ular Lebanese salad. They mixed ingredients in bedpans and turned urinals into flower vases.

They forgot they were in a hospital. They visited back and forth, drinking coffee in each other's rooms as though they were neighbors in an apartment building, planning what to cook for the day and how to share it with others. They brought in bags of potatoes and other vegetables, jars of spices, bottles of oil and other ingredients, and slowly they created mini-homes for their families that provided the luxury of security combined with the basics of water, electricity and cooking fuel. And those who were there for long periods of time felt free in interfering in decisions about what medications patients should be given, when to sedate them and what to feed them, even when the patient was not their own. Sometimes the staff would get irritated with the administration for not putting a stop to all this, but we realized they had little control over the situation. We had to keep remembering that we were living in a lawless society, which demanded that we function with the utmost delicacy and wisdom in trying to maintain our standards in caring for the patients.

Housekeeping deteriorated. How could you keep a hospital clean without a sufficient supply of water? Then there were the mosquitoes and flies that invaded the hospital—even into the operating suites—from the huge piles of uncollected garbage on the streets. The infection rate increased and attempts to curb it called for considerable effort.

It was, in every respect, a horrendous year. Over one period of ten days in February, we treated 474 casualties and 170 were admitted, ranging from simple post-operative care to acute and critical cases. In terms of number per month, our records show four peaks of casualties since 1975: 450 per month in 1975-76; 200 per month in 1981; 1,700 per month in 1982; and 2,000 per month in 1984.

In June, after a temporary lull, hostilities resumed and the Emergency Unit once again was swamped with the

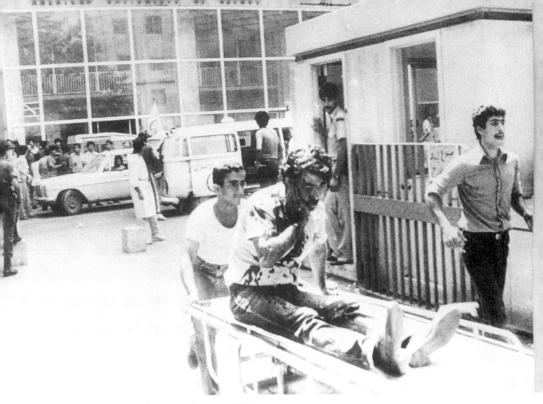

Casualties arriving at the AUBMC Emergency Unit

wounded and the dead. Many of the staff worked double and, during the worst of it, triple shifts around the clock. June 11 alone saw 178 cases, with sixty dead on arrival and fifty-four admissions. Normally, two operating suites were open at night, but that evening all ten were in use, with thirty-one of the surgeries performed within the two hours of 5:30 p.m. to 7:30 p.m. From January to June, AUBMC admitted a total of 1,047 patients. In June alone, we received 462 casualties, with seventy-two dead on arrival and 124 admissions. In token recognition of their efforts, the University gave a twenty-five percent bonus to all those who remained at their posts during the trying month of February.

In July, a ceasefire (another one of so many) was declared, and a security plan was devised to reunify divided Beirut and restore some semblance of order, law,

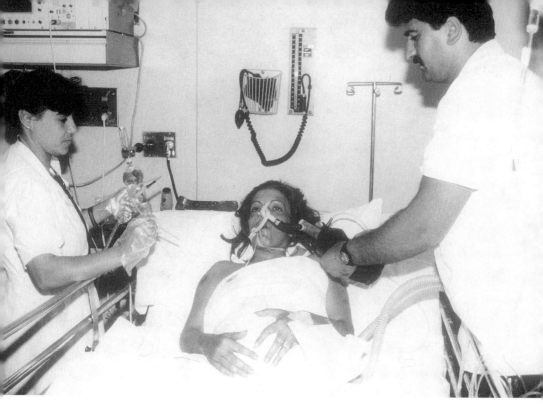

and normalcy to the war-ravaged capital. The airport, which had been shut down, reopened on the morning of July 4 with the arrival of a Middle East Airlines flight from Cyprus. Work on clearing away unexploded shells and mines was initiated. Under Syrian sponsorship, a governmental multi-confessional military council was set up and charged with reintegrating the Lebanese Army, which had split along sectarian lines during the years of conflict. All of this, however, did not signal real peace. On July 2, AUB had to close again because of heavy machine gun fire in the area. Although no one was severely injured, we knew it was not yet time to scatter grains of rice in joy or smile again with sure hope. True, the Lebanese Army was now in control of Beirut and, as the militiamen went home, the guns fell silent. But for how long? And what about all the anger and hatred that still simmered below these surface changes?

AUB, on the whole, was physically in good shape; damage to its buildings through the nine years of destruction was relatively slight. One had only to step through its gates and walk through the campus to see how little it had changed, how beautiful it still was. Outside its walls, in dramatic contrast, lay an ugly, tattered, devastated city.

## Chapter Seven

# Targeting AUB Intensifies

The year 1985 brought with it not only more war casualties but also the renewal of rampant kidnapping and selective killing, the fear of which haunted us all, especially those foreigners still at AUB. The string of tragedies began on May 23, 1985, when Hajj Omar Faour, director of the University's Motor Pool, was killed by a sniper near the Green Line after having safely transported three of our nurses to their homes in East Beirut. In a memorial service held the next day at AUB, more than 1,000 people gathered together to pay their respects to this beloved member of the University family. With their eyes brimming with tears, physicians, professors, nurses, administrators and employees, listened to AUB President Calvin Plimpton deliver the eulogy. Dr. Plimpton said, "He was one of the dearest and the greatest. So many of us have had our lives in his hands and his heart in ours."

Just who was this fifty-eight-year-old man who stood "straight as a ramrod" and of whom Dr. Plimpton said, "He was Lebanon to us"? On paper, Hajj Omar's job seemed

Militiamen roving the streets with their anti-aircraft weapons mundane—he was in charge of the underground parking garage at AUBMC and director of the University's Motor Pool. But, in actuality, Hajj Omar was an indispensable cog in AUB's survival. He was one of those rare individuals who, in the midst of the chaos of war, could find needed supplies, could get people safely to their destination, and who performed these tasks with unfailing optimism, courage and energy.

From the start of the civil war in 1975, Hajj Omar had taken personal responsibility for delivering medical supplies to Beirut hospitals. He would travel daily to Syria to secure oxygen and drugs that were not available in Beirut. When fighting closed the Damascus road via Aley, he would travel through Marjayoun in the south, sometimes making the six-hour trip through treacherous mountain roads twice a day. On one occasion during the heavy clashes in Damour in 1976, Hajj Omar drove a tanker through the fighting to Zahrani to get diesel fuel for the University so that its generators could keep running.

Daily, Hajj Omar transported hospital and AUB personnel across the front lines of the divided city, to and from the airport, to and from Damascus. The joy and relief of seeing him, with his handsome head of white hair, waiting for us at the airport, was indescribable. If a doctor, an administrator or a nurse had to go somewhere, Hajj Omar was always prepared to take him or her, regardless of the risks involved. For example, on August 12, 1982, the day Israeli planes bombed Beirut for twelve hours non-stop, Hajj Omar managed to get the Dean of the Medical School, Dr. Raja Khuri, and Acting President Samir Thabet to an important meeting on the outskirts of Beirut and return them safely to the campus.

Hajj Omar's greatest service to the University was that he offered a sense of security in the midst of chaos. For ten years, he travelled where no one else dared to go. He was not bulletproof, as one physician pointed out, but people had complete confidence in him. During difficult times, they would line up in a convoy behind Hajj Omar, who would lead them across the Green Line. He would drive through the checkpoints with a trail of cars behind him, all of them depending on his skill to get them past the different militia guards. A tall man, full of energy, he gave the impression of unusual size and strength and projected an inner spiritual force that reached out to touch others. After his death, we all thought twice before going to the airport or crossing the Green Line, and with the nurses afraid to trust their lives to anyone else, staff shortage at the hospital increased.

The irony is that after ten years of crossing the most dangerous zones in Lebanon without being hit, a lone sniper bullet felled him. He had good relations with the guards at checkpoints throughout Lebanon and always carried gifts for them. This gave him a mobility that few other people had. He kept track of changing checkpoints and hot spots, and because he travelled to Damascus every day, he always had minute-by-minute updates on the safest roads to use. He would sometimes drive at night without lights to avoid attracting attention, but knew the roads so well that he did not really need lights. Often he would take someone from Beirut to the mountains at one in the morning, return to the city by seven, and take off again the same day for Damascus to get oxygen for the hospital.

A perennial optimist, he always said, "*Kheir Inshallah*" (meaning "Good fortune, God willing"). He had taught his drivers courage, but when the situation was critical he would not let anyone else go. Three days before he died, one of Hajj Omar's drivers was hit by shrapnel; and the day before he was shot, after returning from a run to the airport, he told his son-in-law that he had been afraid to make the trip. It was the only time he admitted fear. I had seen Hajj Omar just a few hours before his death and begged him to stop crossing back and forth, insisting we would manage until the situation improved. He gave me one of his endearing smiles and said, "Do not worry, Miss Mouro, God is with me!" He was truly one of the greatest losses AUB suffered.

One week after Hajj Omar's death, the kidnappings began, one after another. On Tuesday, May 28, David Jacobsen, Director of the Medical Center, was seized. The following day, the body of Denis Hill, an instructor in the University's Intensive English Program, was discovered. He had been shot several times in the head. Hill, who was fifty-three-years-old and a British national, had joined AUB at the start of that academic year and was devoting himself to preparing Lebanon's young men and women for a better future. Yet, just because he was a foreigner, just because he happened to be in the wrong place at the wrong time, he was senselessly killed.

David Jacobsen had just arrived at AUB, the first American in a long time to be appointed hospital director and I reported directly to him. The hospital had begun to return to normal and we looked forward to a new era under his leadership. He would often come to my office and ask to go on rounds with me. He always brought us jellybeans. I remember the day I accompanied him and Joseph Ciccippio, the University's comptroller, on a shopping trip. They wanted to buy some clothing but were hesitant about venturing beyond the safety of the campus, so I volunteered to escort them to the shops nearby. I assumed that being a woman protected me and I felt they were more at risk than I was.

Energetic and committed, Mr. Jacobsen was full of new plans and eager to implement them after so many years of chaos. He needed to work closely with me as the Director of Nursing Services and I thought we made a good team, along with Joe Ciccippio. He had been meeting with staff and with physicians, one by one, and it appeared that he was serious about making changes. He never had the chance.

The fifty-four-year-old Californian was abducted by six gunmen who jumped out of a blue van as he and Dr. Ramez Azouri were crossing the street from campus to the hospital underground parking area. One of the gunmen fired a shot at Dr. Azouri's feet, which luckily only ripped through his trousers, while David Jacobsen was swiftly grabbed, thrown into the van and driven off. No one claimed responsibility for his kidnapping, but at the time AUB and its medical center was controlled primarily by the Amal militia and its PSP allies. The University began making contact with them through its acting president Dr. Lutfi Diab as well as through a public statement released by the medical staff in a concerted effort to secure Jacobsen's release, which read:

> *The Medical Center of the American University of Beirut has continued to provide its services to patients and casualties since the start of troubles in Lebanon, in spite of severe difficulties and risks surrounding the medical staff. The medical faculty announces that it feels that such an act will have a negative effect on medical services at the AUB hospital. We urge the leadership and authorities concerned to assist in releasing Mr. Jacobsen. We also appeal to the kidnappers to free him and to give free scope to doctors and nurses to do their work properly away from all existing conflicts.*

Jacobsen was the second American at AUB to be kidnapped since gunmen began targeting Westerners in July 1982 when Acting President David Dodge was seized. Several days before, unidentified gunmen had abducted two

Frenchmen on the road to the airport. On December 3, 1984, Peter Kilburn, a sixty-year-old University librarian, failed to show up for work. Islamic Jihad, a group of fundamentalist zealots, claimed responsibility for his abduction. Other Americans taken hostage were William Buckley, 56, a U.S. Embassy political officer; and Reverend Benjamin Weir, 60, a Presbyterian minister and father of Chris Weir, who had initiated the hospital's volunteer service. Reverend Weir and his wife had lived and worked in Lebanon for more than thirty years. Also kidnapped were Father Lawrence Jenco, 50, a Roman Catholic priest; and Terry Anderson, 37, the Associated Press correspondent for the Middle East—as if we needed this additional stress. We were to live in a state of fear for years to come.

The University sustained another blow eleven days after Jacobsen was seized. Thomas Sutherland, Dean of the Faculty of Agricultural and Food Sciences, was abducted while coming from the airport. It was as though the kidnapping and killing of foreigners, mainly American and French, was intended to destroy education and research in Beirut. The kidnapping of Reverend Weir, Father Jenco, David Jacobsen, Dr. Sutherland, Peter Kilburn, French researcher Dr. Seurat, the brutal murder of Denis Hill, and the assassination of President Kerr all pointed in one direction. All these individuals had come to Beirut to be of service to the people of Lebanon, a service that the gunmen who kidnapped or murdered them seemed to resent and were determined to undermine.

As for the hijacking of planes, an AUB administrator and his son were hijacked twice in the same day! Dr. Landry Slade, Assistant to the President of AUB, and his sixteen-year-old son William escaped from one hijacking and fell into another one hour later. The Slades were among the passengers of a Royal Jordanian Airlines jet that was taken over on June 11, 1985. They were released with other passengers at the Beirut airport the next day and immediately boarded a Middle East Airlines plane for Cyprus, which in turn was hijacked minutes before reaching Larnaca. However, they were later freed unharmed. How chance governs all!

My fears kept growing that I would be the next kidnap victim. I imagined myself ending up in a room with no lights, tied to a chair for endless nights. I kept reassuring myself that women had not been targeted—maybe because they would be too much of a nuisance. For once, God was on our side—because I was a woman, I would be spared, I thought.

Acting President Raja Khuri announced that the Board of Deans voted unanimously at its meeting on June 10 to cancel commencement ceremonies. After the kidnapping of David Jacobsen, the U.S. State Department issued the following statement:

> *The threat to Americans remains high and no one should consider themselves immune to that threat. We believe that Americans should avoid travel to Lebanon and Americans in Beirut should take advantage of opportunities to leave.*

A previous travel advisory issued by the State Department in 1983 had warned Americans to avoid travelling to Beirut or living there. According to news reports, American diplomats were trying to find a way to end the conflict that had raged on for nine years:

> *We are trying by a variety of diplomatic contacts to explore in Lebanon and other capitals what can be done to bring it to a halt.*

It sure was taking them a long time to bring it to a halt! So what was I to do? Did that mean I should pack up and leave?

More faculty and staff were leaving; foreigners left and the brain drain increased. People were losing hope. I, however, just could not leave the hospital, my so-called "baby." I kept telling myself I was going to survive, no matter what. I was not going to let them scare me off. We were not through yet. The year 1985 was a tough one, and I kept receiving letters from family and friends in the U.S., worrying about my health and safety, pleading with me to be careful, urging me to leave.

On March 11, at 5:15 p.m., a devastating car bomb exploded in West Beirut and more than 100 casualties, most of them females, were rushed to the Emergency Unit. Thirty-four were dead; twenty-five were admitted. Most were burn victims. There was the smell of burnt flesh and the screaming and shouting of people looking for their loved ones. It was all so horrible, like something out of Dante's Inferno. There were so many bodies, stacked one on top of the other. We had run out of stretchers and the morgue had run out of room. The car bomb was meant for a high-ranking Shiite Moslem religious leader. The insane barbarity of such incidents made us fear how it would all end. Would the violence keep spiraling, we wondered, sweeping up in its path more and more innocent victims, like these women and children who happened to be walking past a bomb-rigged car? It could have been any one of us.

One girl, about twelve, who was slightly injured, walked around crying and when I asked her to tell me what was wrong, she said she had been walking with her mother and brother, holding their hands, and suddenly she could not find them anymore. I calmed her with the promise that I would look for her mother and brother, but when I found them, they were both dead, burnt black. How was I going to tell her? I just could not look into those trusting eyes and tell her she would never see her mother or brother again. Fortunately, I found her uncle, who had come to the hospital in search of his relatives. When I gave him the sad news and told him that his niece still did not know, that he would have to take her away from the frightening scene and tell her, he broke down in tears.

The chaos in the Emergency Unit was compounded by the presence of many other people, including hospital employees, who crowded in when they heard and saw the loud commotion that always accompanied the arrival of mass casualties. The security guards could not control them any more than they could the militiamen and their guns, who would even push into the operating rooms.

With each such crisis we tried to improve our handling of the situation so that we would be better prepared for the next one. We assigned specific staff to each area of activity. A senior nurse, together with housekeeping staff and an orderly, were put in charge of dealing with the dead, taking an EKG strip to confirm death. All valuables and personal belongings were removed from the bodies and placed in separate identified envelopes and the senior nurse assigned to this duty would take them to the hospital cashier, where both would sign confirming their delivery and receipt. The floor clerk took the names of all the injured and dead and posted the list outside, where people looking for someone could check the list instead of coming into the Emergency Unit. The Central Supply Department was instructed to extend its hours as needed during a crisis. A stand-by staff in the Dietary Department was there to provide sandwiches for those working in the Emergency Unit, the operating rooms, and the recovery unit. It was my responsibility, helped by a few others, to supervise it all. Last but not least, the morgue technician was asked to sleep in the hospital.

On that night of March 11, twenty operations were performed and seventeen patients remained in the recovery unit overnight. Our Intensive Care Unit had only four beds, and we had to keep several critical patients in the recovery room. Sometimes, post-operative patients had to remain in the recovery unit until patients were discharged from the hospital and beds became available.

Staffing problems continued, with many nurses not reporting for duty during crucial periods. For example, between April 29 and May 31, 1985, the daily percentage rate of absenteeism fluctuated between twelve and forty percent, and only four to eight operating rooms could be kept open. The hospital had approximately five head nurses, twenty-five staff nurses, twenty-nine practical nurses, forty-five aides and six floor clerks: a total of 110 out of a budget of 677. Meanwhile, during the same period, a total of 1,079 casualties were brought into the Emergency Unit, 155 of them dead on arrival. The number of casualties in twenty-four hours jumped from 3 to 146 on May 20 before it began dropping, from 141 (May 22) to 54 (May 24). And the total number of overtime hours expended during that period was 9,077.

It was necessary to meet continually with the hospital administrators, the Chief of Staff and the Dean of the Medical School. At one of our meetings in May 1985, the following decisions were made: (1) Stop all admissions of elective cases. (2) Expedite the discharge of patients to make more beds available. (3) Stop elective heart surgery because of infection risks and also to utilize staff. (4) Expand the Intensive Care Unit from four to nine beds to relieve the Recovery Unit. (5) Have all RNs work a twelve-hour shift, with one day off per week (we needed four RNs per nine patients). (6) Obtain volunteer nurses from other nearby hospitals that could spare staff (many had no emergency facilities and thus did not receive casualties). (7) Look for volunteers among students, mostly in the nursing school, offer to pay them per hour, and assign them as needed and when their studies allowed.

I am sure the reader is wondering why we were still trying to function normally, still trying to fill in the gaps so we could return to admitting elective medical cases, performing elective surgery, and keep classes going at the University. The only alternative would have been to close shop. It was only because of wise decisions on the part of officials, augmented by the hard work and constant dedication of all those who did not abandon ship, that the University and medical center stayed open throughout the fifteen years of war. Had we quit, it would have meant a grievous loss to the country, in both education and medical care.

I continued to receive letters urging me to return to the U.S. One came from Dr. Anne Keane, my advisor in the master's program at the University of Pennsylvania, who wrote: "I am worried about you. I think you should come to the States right away. It's time for you to get out of Lebanon. No one can blame you if you do. When you come here, you should seek some counseling to get over the trauma you've been through."

It was true; I was sinking into a depression. Life had become too much of a struggle. It was too much responsibility, too many pressures. Most of my friends had left and the more depressed I became the more fear I felt that I would be the next kidnap victim. Yet I was determined to go on, even though I knew it was destroying me.

I will never forget Sunday, August 11. At seven in the evening, I was walking on campus with my good friend Asma Farah, who was a head nurse at the hospital. Having given too much of herself, she was no longer able to cope and had finally decided to leave Lebanon. A devoted and conscientious nurse, she had a great deal of untapped potential and wanted to continue her education. Selfishly, I wanted her to stay and help me keep this institution running. I had been losing all my friends, all my best staff, and it was painful. While walking, I was trying to convince her to stay for just one more year and she kept telling me how depressed she was. She could not cope with all the misery and had lost all hope that Lebanon could recover. She was a person of high standards and ideals and could no longer bear to see the hospital deteriorating because of shortages, lack of security, and the exodus of qualified personnel. I had taught her and others like her all I knew and she believed in me. Because of my commitment to AUB and nursing, I wanted to convince her to stay, but my love for her and my conscience stopped me from pressing too hard. In any case, what happened minutes after our discussion, resolved the issue. It is uncanny how often destiny dictates one's future.

We had reached the two benches across the road from Marquand House, where we usually sat for a while to enjoy the beautiful view—the wide expanse of sea and sky, fringed in the north by the dramatic rise of Lebanon's mountains; the verdant slopes of the entire AUB campus leading down to the tennis courts and athletic field below. The benches were about a meter apart and two doctors occupied "our" bench, so we sat on the other and continued our conversation. A few minutes later, the doctors got up and left and two young girls immediately took their place. Just as they sat down, a mortar shell landed nearby and, right in front of our eyes, we saw one girl fly off the bench in one direction and the other in another direction. In a state of shock, Asma and I started running, expecting more shells to follow. Miraculously unharmed, we quickly realized we had to go back to check on the girls. One was already dead, her body completely shattered; pieces of flesh were everywhere, some on our clothing. The other girl was taken to the Emergency Unit in critical condition. They were both sophomore students. Asma and I just sat there shivering in silence, unable to say a word.

That same day, between seven and eight in the evening, we received eighteen casualties from the shelling. The girl we had seen flying through the air had multiple shrapnel wounds and underwent an emergency thoracotomy. Another AUB student was brought in seriously injured, and an hour later someone uselessly showed up with his leg.

Still shaken by the incident and not wanting to be alone, Asma and I went to my apartment. We telephoned her parents to reassure them, then called the Emergency Unit to find out about the injured girl's condition, but it was too soon to get a report. (We later learned that she survived.) We took off our stained and blackened clothes, threw them away and stood under the shower to calm our nerves. We kept asking each other, what if that fateful bench had not been occupied and we had been sitting there as we usually did. I, for one, had lost the will to persuade Asma or anyone to stay in Lebanon. I did not want my dear friend to become another Zeina, Suha, or Jihad who were killed or hurt that day on campus. On the contrary, I contacted the University of Pennsylvania, my alma mater, on her behalf and she was accepted. Asma no longer had any hesitation about leaving, but stubborn Gladys would not be scared off and was even more determined to stay on.

Realizing that the situation was not going to improve, we again re-evaluated our crisis management plan and the Office of Nursing Services arrived at the following decisions: First, we defined the division of labor and assignments in the Emergency Unit. One RN would be assigned to the medical section, another to cover the minor and major surgical areas, and a third to the Outpatient Unit in case of an overflow of casualties. One RN would also be there to prepare tetanus antitoxin and gamma globulin injections for all casualties. One practical nurse would remain in the Pediatric Unit. We would have orderlies on hand at all times—one to assist in the minor and major surgical areas and one to collect, clean and replace used supplies and deliver blood specimens to the laboratory. There would be one floor clerk/receptionist to register all incoming patients. And finally, an orderly or volunteer would be needed to take bodies to the morgue or transport patients to units.

Second, the functions of the nursing supervisor were defined as follows: (1) taking charge of staffing and assignments in the Emergency Unit; (2) verifying death has occurred and supervising removal of valuables, etc.; (3) ensuring the availability of supplies, linens, surgical sets, pharmaceuticals and food; (4) keeping tabs on Emergency Unit identification tags to make sure outsiders were not using them; (5) and assisting security to identify unwelcome visitors and hospital personnel who had no business in the Emergency Unit. The supervisor or Director of Nursing Services would be considered the captain of the emergency ship.

In October 1985, the Medical Dean's office announced that the AUB Motor Pool had organized a weekly convoy to transport those whose homes were in East Beirut. The convoy would depart from AUB every Friday at 2:30 p.m. and return the following Monday at 6:15 a.m., giving staff members the chance to spend the weekend with their families. The convoy would be escorted to guarantee a safe crossing and a bus would be provided for those without cars. Leading the convoy was Abdullah Faour, Hajj Omar's son.

Before she left for the States, Asma had given me a diary

Targeting AUB continues: surveying the damage after an attack

for my birthday. This small black book helped me record my experiences day by day and, for the next five years, became my memory bank.

After David Jacobsen's kidnapping, Joe Ciccippio showed constant concern and would stop by my office every day to check on my welfare, which gave me the chance to unburden myself of all the problems our department was facing. He was one of the few administrators and the only American (besides me) left at AUB, and he was always ready to assist in whatever way he could. Whenever any of the Philippine nurses wanted to return home and needed financial assistance, for example, he helped. He knew I was living off campus and helped me get a larger, safer apartment on campus. At first, I did not like the prospect of living in a big apartment. I was afraid I would feel lonely, especially during shelling, but he encouraged me. With his help, I moved into a beautiful apartment in faculty housing overlooking the sea on January 1, 1986. I decided to have a New Year's Day party to celebrate my move and, I hoped, the beginning of a better year. I invited all my friends from the hospital and it turned out to be the nicest New Year's party we ever had. The situation was fairly calm, no shelling, and we drank and danced until morning. For weeks and months to come, the same group regularly gathered at "Mouro's Place" to unwind. Winters in Lebanon are mild and my balcony was perfect for barbecues, which made for easy entertaining.

May 12, International Nurses Day, was approaching—a day I always made a point of celebrating. Traditionally, nursing in Lebanon (as in most Third World countries) is not the respected profession it is in the States. I wanted to use the day to promote the image of the nurse, to use the war situation to show the community how essential the work of nursing was. This was our day, why not publicize it? We needed more nurses and we needed parents to allow their children to choose nursing as a profession. A public celebration would also improve the morale of our own nurses. So we staged a festival on campus that featured a Philippine folklore show. Our motto for that year was "Unity, Professionalism and Knowledge."

On May 20, AUB's president, Dr. Frederick Herter, who was in Damascus at the time, issued the following statement to the University community:

*I plead with you to go back to teaching, back to classes, back to work. You are endangering the lives of the kidnapped, crippling the education of students and putting in jeopardy the accreditation of the University and its support. Please do not allow the University to close.*

The next two months of June and July were more or less calm. We took every advantage of the temporary stability to relax and enjoy life for a change. Yet, one by one, the friends that met at "Mouro's Place" began to leave Lebanon. The group used to laugh that Gladys would be the last one left in Lebanon, sitting on a tank and waving the Lebanese and American flags. They knew I was not going to leave under any circumstances.

I reproached them for leaving. Who would take care of the people here who needed them? I could not accept the fact that they could not wait until the war ended, that they wanted to get on with their lives, make a future for themselves elsewhere and maybe, just maybe, come back to Lebanon again to rebuild their country. But most of them did not come back; life in the States was too good—and so safe.

It was getting lonelier and lonelier for me and my depression increased. Joe Ciccippio was a great support and often took me to the president's office, where there was a direct international line, to telephone my family and friends in the U.S. Although the situation was relatively calm, that year of 1986 brought with it another kind of danger that became not only life threatening but also very damaging to the academic and medical standards of AUB and the hospital. The two political factions in control of West Beirut—Amal and the PSP—began penetrating our operational structure, intimidating their way into positions of authority as professors, doctors, interns and the like. And as they began throwing their weight around, we found ourselves literally living under a dictatorship. Students dissatisfied with their grades threatened professors; patients and their families demanding priority attention or expecting miracles in medical care threatened doctors and nurses.

After David Jacobsen's kidnapping, the Acting

Hospital Director who took his place, Ahmad Nasrallah, was rumored to belong to the Amal party. He was an AUB graduate who had been sent to the U.S. for a master's degree by a previous hospital director and, upon his return, had been appointed assistant director. He happened to be in the right place at the right time and in the right position. I, for one, was not very happy about his promotion to acting director. He became my direct boss and, because of his strong political backing, I had to be careful in dealing with him if I expected to remain alive. I decided it would be wise not to oppose him. So, with Ciccippio's help, I established a fairly good relationship with him.

Gradually, the pressures began. I would get a phone call to employ this or that person, and if I said no, I was often threatened. On September 12, 1986, I was in the operating room when I overheard someone say, "They kidnapped Mr. Ciccippio!" I could not believe it. I went directly to the acting director to find out if it was true. He confirmed it and added that he did not know who was responsible. I could not believe it. Nasrallah knew all the political factions, certainly he could do something about it. I went on a verbal rampage. "Why," I screamed at him, "Why? Wasn't he helping the poor? Wasn't he a good guy? Didn't he support you? Is it because he didn't convert to Islam and fast for Ramadan!" But deep down I knew there would be no getting him back.

The day before, Ciccippio and I had been drinking coffee and he told me he would not leave until I left. Now he was cruelly taken away, seized by force at half past six in the morning right near the building where we both lived, just fifteen minutes before I left for work. Why had he not listened to everyone and left Lebanon? I had lost my best friend and felt guilty, lonely and afraid. It took me a long time to get over his kidnapping. I could not sleep and was plagued by nightmares.

As the days went by, I became more and more depressed. I began taking pills, some to numb the pain, others to find escape in hours of deep dreamless sleep. I lost energy, became apathetic and began shortening my work hours. I, Gladys Mouro, responsible for a staff of hundreds, had to resort to antidepressants and sleeping pills. What would people say? What would my nurses say—I, who was supposed to support them, boost their morale, give them advice on how to cope? Did it mean I was finally giving up? And yet, kidnappings or no kidnappings, pills or no pills, I only knew that I would not leave. My dedication to my profession, my stubborn commitment to AUB, and my ego, would not let me give up.

I spent Christmas Day in bed watching television, not able to face anyone or anything, fearing I would be tempted to take more pills. I did not know what to do. I was totally lost, feeling profound sadness about something and not knowing what it was, needing someone to lean on, but being too proud to admit it. There was no fighting at the time and as I look back I realize I was experiencing post-traumatic depression, a letting go of all the pent-up stress, fear and sorrow of the past years, just as the 1983 conference on mental health had warned.

Friends like Nayla Zurayk would write:

> *…hang in there…they need you, all those nurses and patients…. We all admire your courage and, more often than not, we understand how you feel.*

Others, like Susan Gouthier, would implore me to leave:

> *Why are you putting up with all this in Lebanon? I know this question could be answered with one*

Escape: women flee the shelling

*word—dedication—but to whom? What good will
you be if something terrible happens to you? In the
final analysis, survival is all that matters.*

And my brother George wrote:

*I think, Gladys, the time has come for you to leave
Lebanon. Lebanon will never get back to what it was
and you should not put yourself through this agony.
All of your friends have left and your continued support of AUB is over and beyond the call of duty.*

Did they really understand how I felt? When you invest
so much of yourself in something, when you realize how
much you are still needed, it is not easy to walk away.
At times I felt anger towards those friends who had left

and wanted me to leave too. I will show them, I would say to myself, but showing them plunged me further into depression. My department was slowly dying; the best of our nursing staff had left and many of the senior nursing students began applying for positions abroad even before graduation. Each day I would drag myself to work reluctantly. Even the news that David Jacobsen had been released failed to give me hope. Joe Ciccippio was still held and others were still being kidnapped.

The hospital was receiving casualties sporadically. The militias, still in control, were imposing their will left and right. It was not easy to make rounds without interference of some kind. Visitors, especially the militiamen, were rude and thought they owned the world. Fortunately, few of the nurses were politically involved, or at least they did not flaunt it. All the nursing staff maintained a professional attitude and I tried my best to help them in strengthening the hospital's standards of service.

By the end of 1986, the medical school had a new dean, Dr. Adnan Mroueh, but my nemesis, the Acting Hospital Director, was still hovering over me.

## Chapter Eight
# Personal Threats Increase

In West Beirut, 1987 turned out to be another hallmark year of deprivation, suffering and fear. Not so in East Beirut, where the militias coordinated in organizing many public services, neighborhood by neighborhood, and where the people felt more protected and secure. The atmosphere there was lively, almost frenetic, with restaurants and nightclubs doing a brisk business. I crossed over one weekend with friends and attended a show featuring the well-known singer Majida Roumy. It was so wonderful and yet so sad and surrealistic, all this gaiety against the backdrop of violence and death that continued to hang over our heads.

On January 6 another round of fierce fighting erupted between Amal and the PSP. Again, staff failed to show up for work; again, electricity was cut off; and again, casualties poured into the hospital. Meanwhile, both parties continued to pressure me to hire their people. One was an orderly, a member of the PSP, who was in the Practical Nursing Program and wanted a permanent position in the hospital. He was aggressive, totally brainwashed by his party and a tool in their hands. He was always armed, carried a walkie-talkie, and every time we had casualties he was there looking out for the interests of his party. I stood firm and refused to employ him. I knew that if it was left to other department heads, they would have hired him and spared themselves—and their families—the consequences of turning him down. I thought differently. Maybe it was because I had no family in Beirut to worry about. Maybe I looked upon it as one more challenge in my determination to maintain standards in spite of every-thing. Maybe it was pure stubbornness or rash defiance against those who wanted to take over or destroy AUB and its medical center.

One of our interns asked me to employ two practical nurses who were known to be involved in political parties. When I refused, telling him they were not competent, he went to the Dean. I told the Dean I had already made my decision and asked him to let me handle it. Was it foolish? I was so angry to have to deal with such rubbish. What fol-lowed, of course, was a threatening phone call from the intern. Two years later, the same two practical nurses were hired after I found out they were no longer party members. One was later killed and the other left for the United Arab Emirates. That intern is now an attending surgeon at AUBMC. One day, when we chanced to meet in the hospital, he stopped me and said, "Gladys, I am proud of how you handled the situation. When we are young, we tend to make mistakes and do things that are not right." It felt good to hear him acknowledge his wrongdoing and appreciation for the position I had taken.

In spite of the increasing pressure, I would not give in. Party leaders tried to scare me into resigning so they could replace me with one of their own. They left notes under my door intended to frighten me, threatening me with death if I did not bow to their wishes. Friends escorted me on all trips beyond the campus and hospital, wherever I went. Day by day, the nightmare of constant fear continued. Nasrallah, while appearing to be an objective and just hospital administrator, remained politically active. I knew this and yet had no choice but to accept it. Nevertheless, I started having problems with him as, more and more, he tried to convince me to employ politically affiliated people. I took one or two at the most, but I closely monitored their behavior and made it clear that they were expected to meet standards. It became almost impossible to take a firm stand against the pressure and, increasingly, people who were not competent were hired. Even students who were not qualified were admitted to the University. Thank God, this situation did not last long or it would have been catastrophic for AUB and the medical center.

Everyone in a responsible position felt threatened. With families to think about, they either accommodated or quit their jobs. Professors and doctors left or sent their families away. During that year I was offered the position of Director of Nursing with an attractive salary at a hospital in Qatar. But I turned it down, even though I knew I was losing an ideal opportunity to end my life of fear and at the same time continue to pursue my professional aspirations. I just did not want to give up on Lebanon.

On January 12, at one in the morning, my telephone rang. Always afraid of telephone calls in the middle of the night, I almost did not answer it. It was an unknown voice, a man, asking me to come down to the gate and identify my car. "Why?" I asked. "What happened? Who are you?" He said, "I'm from University Security and someone has put a piece of dynamite under your car. It almost went off. You are lucky we caught it in time. We need you to come down." My God, I thought to myself, what if the dynamite had been rigged to go off when I started the car? Or timed to go off before daylight, before anyone noticed anything? The car was a cheery yellow 1976 Fiat, the very first car I had ever owned and I was so proud of it. My next thought was that maybe it was a trick, maybe that man really is not a security guard, and maybe it is someone with kidnapping on his mind. Afraid to go down alone, I called two doctor friends at the hospital, told them the story and asked them to accompany me to the gate where the car was parked. They came quickly and the three of us went down. The security guard, a soldier I had never seen before, asked me if the Fiat was my car. I nodded, unable to utter a word. The gate man, who was on his rounds when he happened to notice the fuse under the car, had courageously disconnected it from the dynamite.

To put it mildly, my situation had become serious. Someone wanted to kill me or at least scare me out of Beirut. I was not the right person for the nursing director's position. "They" wanted someone else with more flexibility. I was resisting any change that was not compatible with the principles of AUB and the nursing profession, so "they" decided to do all they could to get rid of me. But who? At that point I simply could not remain at home alone and at 3:00 a.m. went with my friends to the hospital to sleep in the security of my office, despite its discomforts.

At eight in the morning I reported the incident to the Acting Hospital Director. Who else could I turn to? He was my boss and the proper channel of communication, even though I knew deep down he could not care less for my welfare. Maybe he even knew it was planned. After all, Ciccippio, who he appeared to hold in high regard and swore to protect, had been kidnapped; and Jacobsen, whom he had escorted everywhere, was also kidnapped. And he claimed he could do nothing to secure their release. So why would he be concerned about my safety? He was not. When I told him, he just brushed it off as a minor incident not to be taken seriously. I felt so insecure and frightened, as though surrounded by a pack of wolves ready to pounce on me.

Threats against me, oral and written, continued throughout the month, prompting the entire nursing staff, from clerks to RNs, to write the following letter to the hospital administration:

*On Monday, January 12, at 1:00 a.m., Miss Gladys Mouro was informed by the AUB Security Office that a TNT charge timed to explode was placed under her car, near her faculty apartment on AUB premises (the car was marked for identification). Fortunately the guard noted the explosive in time and the dynamite was disconnected. Hospital administration was informed the same day.*

*From January 12 up until the present date (January 21), Mr. Kamal Farhat, a temporary hospital employee, has been openly threatening and cursing various senior nursing and medical personnel, particularly Miss Mouro, whom he has been repeatedly harassing and threatening over the past two years). Again, hospital administration was approached.*

*On Monday, January 19, a note reading, 'You are going to die,' was placed under the door of Miss Mouro's office. The nursing staff called for another meeting with the administration. Mr. Ahmad Nasrallah promised to take appropriate measures. Up until this date, no concrete measures have been taken.*

*As a nursing body, we feel that any threat against the Nursing Services Director is a threat against all nursing personnel. Therefore, we demand:*

*1) An active involvement of the hospital adminis-tration in this security problem.*

*2) The permanent removal of Mr. Kamal Farhat from the hospital and AUB premises.*

*We feel no serious consideration has been given to this matter. We expect a reply by 12:00 noon, Thursday, January 22.*

Fifteen nursing supervisors signed the letter and copies were sent to the Acting President of AUB, Lutfi Diab and several top level University and hospital officials. The Acting Hospital Director looked upon the letter as an insult, considered it a personal attack and, of course, did nothing. The nurses then threatened to go on strike if nothing was done. I tried to calm them down and succeeded in convincing them not to strike. I informed Nasrallah of my role in preventing the strike, but this act of concern for the hospital's continued existence apparently made no difference to him. He began taking revenge on me for the letter in any way he could to make my life even more miserable than it was. On one occasion, when I told him I could not attend a meeting because I was under tremendous stress he reprimanded me in an official letter stating, "Stress on a senior management person should not lead to insubordination," and sent copies of it to the Acting Dean and the Personnel Director. I was furious to get such a letter, especially after all my services to him and to the hospital. I realized more than ever how much he wanted to get rid of me.

The hospital security committee, composed of doctors and members of the Security Department, asked me if I wanted a bodyguard. I refused, believing it would just make the situation more obvious and knowing also that it would not do much good. Our security guards could not even keep the problem orderly Farhat away from the hospital. He belonged to a strong political party that wanted him to stay around the hospital to gather information. For a long while, I avoided driving and later, every time I started my car, I would do so with a prayer. I would not let friends ride with me. I walked to work and cut down on any excursions beyond AUB. The nightmare of fear continued for the next three years until all hostages were released and the war finally ended.

In 1990, to my great relief, Farhat moved to Switzerland. A few years later, while in Lebanon, he came to visit me and said he was sorry for what had happened in the past, that he realized that I had acted for the good of the hospital. I guess these people really did not know what they were doing at the time. Vulnerable and hungry for attention, they were trapped in a cauldron of chaos, violence, pressure and brainwashing.

On January 13, 1987, when one of the house staff was kidnapped, the Emergency Unit in response closed its doors. He was released immediately. That was when I decided to get myself a gun. I learned how to use it and kept it loaded in my purse all day and under my pillow at night. It gave me a strong sense of security, even though I knew I was no match for all the professional gunmen around. I knew that at any moment, any one of them could easily kill me. But it seems they had put that option on hold and decided to concentrate instead on trying to scare me away, which in itself was a daily torture.

I later found out how a friend of mine, who was in the States and worried about my safety, helped keep me alive. Before the war, she had been a close friend with a man who later became one of the leaders of the party to which Farhat belonged. When she heard of the threats on my life, she contacted her friend and asked him to take care of me and not let anyone harm me. She told me that he once remarked, "Gladys is too idealistic and stuck to principles. She must be more flexible." Had it not been for his promise to her, I might have been dead by now. That same man was later appointed a minister in the Lebanese government.

Despite her help, despite all the reassurances of support I received from University and hospital officials, I continued to live in a constant state of fear. Frightening dreams continued to jolt me out of sleep at night and I began developing abdominal pains induced by anxiety. Joe Ciccippio's wife, Ilham, who worked at the American Embassy, called to warn me to leave Lebanon and said she was asked to leave because the situation had become too dangerous. When they heard about the dynamite under my car, my family threatened to come to Cyprus and evacuate me by force if I did not leave. My brother George was the one I respected and listened to most and I did not want him to get upset with me, but at the same time, I just could not leave.

To add to my problems, my residence permit to remain in Lebanon now had to be renewed every three months instead of once a year. It was about to expire and I was getting desperate. How was I going to stay? The only alternatives were to get forged papers, which I categorically rejected, or to marry a Lebanese—which I gave some thought to, I must admit. It would not have been difficult to find a Lebanese willing to marry me. So many were dying to go to the U.S. and become American citizens. Ironically, I was probably the only one around interested in getting a Lebanese residence card. I had several offers of marriage, but I just could not take that step. There was no way I could accept marrying someone just to secure a residence permit. No matter what, I had to hold on to my principles. Besides, it could very well turn out to be a jump from the frying pan into the fire. Suppose that person later turned around and, as sometimes happens, blackmailed me?

On January 31 U.S. Secretary of State George Shultz issued a complete travel ban on Lebanon stating that

> …*effective immediately U.S. passports are <u>not</u> valid for travel to, in and through Lebanon unless specifically valid for such travel. We are granting a class exception of up to 30 days for citizens currently in Lebanon so that they may use their passports to depart without violating the law. We are also granting a class exception to the immediate family members of hostages. All other exceptions will be decided on a case by case basis. Violators of these passport controls will be subject to prosecution. It should be clear that while the U.S. government will attempt to help its unlawfully detained citizens in Lebanon or elsewhere, our ability to secure their release is limited both by the chaos in Lebanon and our responsibility to protect broad national interests, including the avoidance of action which might encourage future acts of terrorism. This determination is not lightly made. We are loathe to impede the travel of American citizens in any way. Nevertheless, the situation in Lebanon and in West Beirut in particular, is so chaotic that we do not believe any American citi-*

*zen can be considered safe from terrorist*
*acts....Therefore, the Secretary is exercising his*
*authority to invalidate U.S. passports to, in and*
*through Lebanon in an effort to persuade Americans*
*not to go or remain in Lebanon.*

Fortunately, I had renewed my passport in 1985 and it would be valid for eight more years. When I requested to remain in Lebanon, Dr. Frederick Herter, AUB's president, as well as top hospital officials, wrote letters to support my petition. U.S. Ambassador Richard Murphy replied that the State Department would not make an exception in my case. If I remained in Lebanon, I would have to pay the $2000 fine. Imagine paying a fine for doing a good deed! I wanted a break and missed my family, but I could not take the risk. Suppose I could not get back to Lebanon? So I took my chances and stayed.

On February 9 fighting erupted again between the PSP and Amal and thirty casualties were brought into the Emergency Unit. On February 18 we received 130 casualties. That night, I spent two hours in the underground parking shelter. The problem orderly was still around, carrying guns and a walkie-talkie. The fighting finally stopped when the Syrian Army entered Beirut on February 21. How I continued to cope, I do not know. Emotionally, physically and psychologically, I was drained. I prayed to God to give me strength and courage.

The year continued with its ups and downs. I managed to get a United Nations passport to facilitate my comings and goings. It would give me a chance to travel elsewhere and still return to Lebanon. On May 12, to celebrate Nurses' Day, I organized a panel discussion on the nursing image. On June 2 Prime Minister Rashid Karami was assassinated. On June 19 the American journalist Charles Glass was abducted in the Ouzai area. He was the ninth American to be kidnapped.

Dr. Ibrahim Salti was appointed Deputy President of AUB to represent Dr. Herter, who remained in New York. AUB held its graduation ceremonies, but not outdoors on the athletic field (known as the Green Field), but within the safer confines of the Assembly Hall. Water, electricity and gasoline were still in short supply. Inflation was rampant. My monthly salary was the equivalent of $150 (in 1986, fifty Lebanese pounds equalled one dollar; by 1987, 300 Lebanese pounds amounted to one dollar).

Dr. Samir Najjar, Chairman of the Department of Pediatrics for several years and presently Dean of the Medical School, wrote the following in the 1987 winter issue of the AUB Newsletter:

> *Many times, it was difficult for us to reconcile our long hours of attention to the care of a single child, when dozens more were maimed or killed in a matter of seconds. Evidence of the adverse impact of the violence stems from three sources—common sense, anecdotes and scientific study. Common sense tells us that children in Lebanon have suffered immensely. Common sense also tells us that children in Lebanon live in great fear—fear for their safety and that of their loved ones, fear of the terrible noises from the latest armaments, and fear from the tales of horror and wild rumors that circulate.*

Dr. Najjar went on to say how the children in Lebanon have been denied the recreational activities usually taken for granted. Confined to their homes for days on end, only the fortunate had television to fall back on, but that too had its drawbacks, with so many programs unsuitable for children. Worst of all, thousands of youths joined the militias, some as young as ten. One physician sent his son to Paris to get him away from the violence—where he spent much of his time drawing pictures of guns, tanks and explosions. Naturally, the incidence of psychosomatic ailments among children increased. Dr. Harout Armenian, former Dean of the Faculty of Health Sciences, initiated an interdisciplinary project to assess the condition of children in Lebanon after a decade of war. The project involved AUB educators, physicians, psychologists, sociologists, economists and public health professionals. Summarized in Dr. Armenian's book *The State of Children in Wartime*, the results of the study cover six areas: physical health, mental health, environmental conditions, social environment, economic activity and schooling. There was no doubt that the war adversely affected children, but the question was how severely and how permanently? Even those fortunate enough to escape physical harm were affected psychologically. So many of them suffered repeated upheaval and frequent displacement which stunted their educational, cultural and social development in varying degrees, depending on the emotional integrity of the family and its ability to cope with traumatic situations. While it is easy to measure the physical harm inflicted, it is difficult to assess the duration and severity of the psychological scars.

Dr. Mounir Shamaa, professor of Internal Medicine (who was briefly abducted during the early years of the war and is still on the AUB staff), had this to say about the effects of the war in the winter issue of the AUB newsletter:

*In my medical practice I am encountering more bonafide cases of anxiety, depression, hysterical behavior and exaggerated emotional expressions than ever before. People on the streets do not smile anymore. Moreover, attitudes towards death have been greatly affected. In the past, death was a*

*calamity. Now, because of its frequency and famil-
iarity, death has become an uneventful occur-
rence—particularly if it is due to natural causes.
Violence registers only when it happens to you or
to your immediate neighbor. If it emits two blocks
away, however, it goes unnoticed.*

In August a temporary floor clerk who was a member of the PSP began telephoning me at home, threatening to kill me. In September, I received a letter from him, pressuring me to employ him permanently. I refused. For a while it was a living nightmare; wherever I went, I saw him. I would wake up in the middle of the night imagining a gun pointed at my head. Even patients were at risk. One of our nursing supervisors reported that she saw a man go into a patient's room and put a pistol to the patient's head. Fortunately, voices over the hospital paging system scared him and he rushed out of the room. We never knew the reason for the attack. Occasionally unknown parties would snatch a corpse from the morgue without authorization.

On the morning of Saturday November 14, around forty-five minutes past eleven, while in my car driving to the hospital I heard a radio news flash reporting an explosion in the hospital near the cashier's office. I rushed there and entered from the basement. The power was off, all was pitch dark and everyone was in panic, not knowing what to do. Seven people had been killed and thirty-seven injured. A woman carrying a box of chocolates had entered the hospital and sat on a bench near the cashier's office, when suddenly the box blew up. Who? Why? No one knew. We had hunches. Could it be to show everyone that the Syrians really did not have control of the country? A similar incident had occurred at the airport. The walls of the hospital lobby had collapsed. Intestines and flesh hung from the ceiling; shoes, papers, money, sticks of furniture and human limbs were scattered everywhere. My office, its door blasted open, was full of broken glass. Had it been a weekday more lives would have been lost. My secretary Joumana stood there terrified; she had seen the cashier hurt—but miraculously not killed. Did the woman with the box of chocolates know what she was carrying; did she know she was going to die? I later saw her body in the morgue. It was cut in half. I remembered seeing her before in the hospital, but never knew who she was. She was never identified.

Sitting in my office was May Shibbani, a practical nurse who worked in the operating room. When she saw me she burst into tears. She had just heard that her sister, who was twenty-five years old and two months pregnant, and her husband were among the dead. The poor woman had been in the hospital for observation, but had persuaded her physician to discharge her and was at the cashier's office with her husband to pay her bill when the bomb went off. The couple left a three-year-old child behind. A seventeen-year-old International College student, who had been to visit her uncle in the Coronary Care Unit, also died. A mother, who was carrying her baby when she heard the explosion, became petrified and dropped the infant on the floor. Fortunately, a nurse nearby who saw what had happened quickly scooped up the baby and took it to the nursery.

One week later all was "back to normal." Windows were replaced, doors were fixed and electricity was restored. Only the bench upon which the woman with her box of chocolates had been sitting was totally gone. It was hard to imagine targeting an institution that had served so many people throughout twelve years of war, irrespective of race, religion or political affiliation. Why the hospital? President Amin Gemayel paid tribute to the Medical Center as "an institution that has never stopped serving patients of all factions, without discrimination." The U.S. State Department strongly condemned "the contemptible and heartless crime that aimed at promoting terrorism." And, at the hospital, several measures were taken to tighten security. Visiting hours were restricted, with only two visitors per patient at a time; all visitors were to be searched; no food, flowers or gifts would be allowed; and no person would be permitted to enter the AUB campus without an official University identification card.

Family and friends called to make sure I was okay. And my brother George, whom I expected to increase his pressures on me to leave, wrote the following in a letter I received from him soon afterwards:

> *Gladys, I envy you, because you are living a life of excitement, rewarding, and above all helping those who are in need. You have done what most of us only dream of. You are like the nurses, doctors and humanitarians that go to places of danger like Afghanistan, who risk their lives to help people, putting themselves in danger and working twenty hours a day. I would love to be there with you. I, too, would go. Keep it up, stay with it and do your thing. I and others are behind you.*

Finally, he was convinced that I had made the right decision. I also received an invitation to the Ph.D. graduation of my friend Huda Ayyash in the States and experienced a brief moment of regret that I had not pursued the same course.

Still plagued by the severe nursing shortage, we launched a campaign to improve the image of nursing, with the hope

of encouraging more students to enter the profession. The media campaign included television interviews with nurses to highlight the gratifying rewards of a career in nursing. It was strange to be involved in such activities in the middle of a war, but life went on. We needed to develop a steady supply of nurses and the recruiting activity was one way of diverting our efforts to something worthwhile for the future. Meanwhile, no one knew when the war would end.

The aftermath of the
chocolate-box bomb in
the AUBMC lobby

## Chapter Nine
# The Tough Get Going

The year 1988 began as a more or less quiet one and I found time to implement a project I had put on hold for several years. I wanted to open a daycare center for those nurses who had nowhere to leave their children, believing it would encourage them to return to work and, thus, help alleviate the nursing shortage. For me, it was an exciting and pleasurable project. I had no children of my own, and the idea of starting a nursery, planning a childcare program, buying equipment and toys for children intrigued me.

What a wonderful day it was when we opened the center—on March 21, Lebanese Mother's Day—with six children, their mothers and dozens of the nursing staff filling the room in happy, boisterous celebration. I was so proud. At last, amid all the madness we had been living, I was able to do something that made sense. The center was located in the hospital and, by 1994, was accommodating thirty-five children—not only those of nurses but also the children of doctors, secretaries and other hospital personnel.

Surveying the damage of
a car bomb explosion

In early May, these momentary dreams of better days ahead were dashed by the sudden eruption of new battles—this time between a new set of adversaries, Amal and Hizbullah (Party of God). We received fifty casualties the first day from both groups and our overriding fear was that they would continue their fighting in the hospital. On Saturday, May 14, when thirteen casualties were operated on, only five of our operating rooms were open because of lack of personnel. Most of our practicals and orderlies were from the danger areas and only four were able to report for duty.

At the last minute we were forced to postpone our annual celebration of International Nurses' Day on May 12—but only temporarily. We later planned and organized a health fair, which included booths related to staff development, nursing audit, ambulatory services, critical care units, medical units, surgical units, equipment, book sales and others. Our 1988 motto was "When the going gets tough, the tough get going."

In my Nurses' Day address I emphasized the critical nature of our nursing shortage. I spoke of some of the solutions we had resorted to that year. How we affiliated with the Lebanese Red Cross, although it was based on the French medical system. How we employed nurses from other hospitals and schools and gave them courses in English and medical terminology. How we created a preceptor program to orient new graduates and nurses coming from outside AUB. How we offered scholarships to students who chose to pursue a BS in nursing. How we provided transportation and provided three meals daily, as well as housing facilities, to all RNs. How we undertook a media campaign to encourage nursing as a career. And, finally, how we established our daycare center.

I told my nurses that I wanted them to remain strong, to express their views and insist on their rights, but I also admitted that I myself found it difficult at times to practice what I preached. How can one motivate people who feel their lives constantly at risk, who often find themselves serving without financial reward or appreciation for their work? How can one tell those living in an atmosphere of hopelessness, violence, hatred and stress to be loyal to their profession—especially when that profession is not given the respect it deserves from the society it serves? Because this respect has been so often lacking in Lebanon and the Arab world, too few young people have been inclined to choose nursing as a profession. This must change. Nurses need to be recognized and appreciated for the vital services they render. To improve the public image of nursing as a highly respected and valued profession will require persistent effort. Nurses need to be recognized and appreciated for their vital contributions to the well-being of society. It is extremely difficult these days to hold tight to the Florence Nightingale ideal, where service, self-sacrifice and loyalty become rewards in themselves, but we must continue to do so. There is no other alternative. Be proud of yourselves. Without nurses, hospitals fall and all people suffer. Let us all join hands to give nursing the honorable stature it deserves. As Aristotle said, "A common danger unites the bitterest enemies and a common arrow is easily broken, but not ten in a bundle."

I concluded with these words, "If I now had a glass of wine, I would drink a toast to you all. You kept this institution running. Be proud of yourselves... I wish you all a Happy Nurses' Day. May we have nurses next year and have them more abundantly."

In August I was invited to be the keynote speaker at a talk on trauma in nursing at the Third International

Intensive Care Nursing Conference in Montreal. At first, I worried about leaving Lebanon—I wanted to visit the States after the conference but feared U.S. immigration would fine me and not let me return to Lebanon. I decided, however, to take that chance and worry about whatever would happen when it happened. At the conference, before an audience of almost 2,000 professionals, I outlined the various aspects of nursing management in situations of trauma and also talked about some of my personal experiences. I was overwhelmed by the standing ovation I received; I later learned that my talk had received the highest rating of all those presented at the conference. I also received the following letter from one of the conference participants:

> I had the privilege of attending your address to
> the Third International Intensive Care Nursing
> Conference in Montreal. My fellow AACN Western
> New York Chapter members, friends from New
> York and many other conference attendees were
> deeply moved by your presentation. I fear that the
> superficial media coverage of the war that many
> of us depend on for information has desensitized
> many North Americans. Your portrayal made the
> effects of the war on the people of Lebanon
> painfully clear. Nurses in the States take many
> things for granted. We assume and expect that
> our basic safety needs will be met. We cherish our
> political system, but I fear that we take the benefits
> of the stability it brings for granted. We are rich in
> resources and talent and yet too often we cry out
> for more. You made us stop and think. You showed
> us a proud people, a beautiful land that is now
> ravaged by war. You told us of ordinary nurses

*whose courage, bravery and dedication revealed extraordinary people. I am not a great writer, but I am rarely at a loss for words. However, your address left me speechless. I find this letter difficult to write. How can one respond to such a need? How can we help our peers in Lebanon? Let me thank you for telling us of your struggle. Your efforts inspire us all.*

With the conference behind me I prepared for the great adventure of going home. I thought that instead of flying from Montreal to Boston and having to pass through airport immigration, I would take the bus down. I was using my U.S. passport and was worried. It was a nice drive, but I was too tense to enjoy it. I had books with me and planned to tell the immigration officer I was studying in the States. Almost trembling with anxiety, I began perspiring as I approached immigration. But, miracle of miracles, nothing happened. It was over before I knew it and I was now in the land of my birth. It was wonderful to see my family and friends, but also somewhat disturbing. Most of them kept asking me why I was so determined to return to Lebanon after all that I had gone through. No matter what I said, I just was not able to make them understand.

I spent a few days visiting hospitals to see what was going on in American nursing. There were so many new trends in education and technology. The issues they were concerned with seemed so trivial and irrelevant to me, thinking of Lebanon and how we were just trying to survive and treat patients. Documentation was so important to them; at AUB we hardly had time to breathe, let alone be concerned with documentation. I realized how much I had missed and tried to make the most of my stay by gathering whatever information I could to take back and share with my nurses. I did not want the war to deny us knowledge. I did not want my staff to feel completely isolated from mainstream developments in nursing. Once the miserable fighting ended, we would have much catching up to do.

On my return to the land of chaos and violence, fearing I would be denied entry, I decided not to enter through the Beirut airport but elected instead to come back via Cyprus and through the port of Jounieh on the east side of Beirut. My plane ticket read New York/ Amsterdam/Larnaca, Cyprus, which avoided any suspicious questions from immigration as to my final destination. My visa for Lebanon was waiting for me in Jounieh, thanks to the help of a highly placed religious official I knew, as were the friends who met my boat and drove me back to AUB.

I returned to work the next day. Nothing had improved. The atmosphere of shelling, shooting and looting had not evaporated in my absence, and it was difficult to deal with staff. Most of them were support personnel and they resisted my attempts to impose discipline. Thefts in the hospital were increasing. And again, after my brief hiatus of peace and pleasure in the U.S., I fell back into a pattern of depression. I tried to relieve the stress by playing tennis, but it did not always help.

To add to my responsibilities, Dean Mroueh asked me to develop a three-year Baccalaureate Technical (BT) nursing diploma program. The nursing shortage was as severe as ever and the idea was to have AUB produce more nurses instead of having to continue to recruit them from abroad. It was a huge challenge; I had almost no experience in nursing education. The School of Nursing, which had already refused to adopt this three-year program, offered no assistance or support. The ideal, of course, would have been to increase enrollment in the School of Nursing's four-year BS program. But often the BS graduates left Lebanon to work elsewhere and, even without that drain, the demand remained much greater than the school could fill.

It was not easy to start the BT program from scratch with no support, no classrooms and no staff. I asked questions and learned and, with the help of my staff plus an extraordinary measure of persistence, we launched the program. It was not easy to find qualified applicants. Local high school standards had deteriorated, especially in teaching the English language—and the BT program, like all courses at AUB, was to be taught in English. Few students were seriously motivated. They were impoverished children of the war and viewed nursing as no more than a way to earn a living. But, after concentrated efforts at publicizing the program throughout the country, we were able to enroll twenty students. And in February 1989, with hardly anyone to teach or help, we began classes. With the help of nurses on the floor and out of practically nothing, we graduated our first class of twelve BT nurses in July 1991. Since then a total of ninety students have graduated. They have scored as top nursing technicians in Lebanon and are keeping up with their BSN colleagues. Most of them work at the AUB Medical Center and, time and again, have prevented units from closing.

The BT program is funded by AUB—the students pay no tuition, which has helped attract students. These young people, who knew only war, intolerance and hatred, are being trained in more than patient care; they are being taught teamwork, discipline and commitment. They are being molded into nursing professionals who will not only serve the hospital and the community at large, but also themselves in their aspirations for the future.

Expanding the corps of nurses in Lebanon has always been a problem. There are, in fact, more doctors than there are nurses in Lebanon. Even with its limitations, the BT program is helping alleviate that shortage. What can we do when someone with a BSN degree spends a few months at the hospital and then says that she has found a more attractive opportunity elsewhere? U.S. hospitals, which also face a nursing shortage, have been attracting our RNs with good salaries, a green card and a one-way ticket. I remember the time when a nurse recruiter from the U.S. showed up in Cyprus to interview our graduates. I considered it highly unethical to recruit nurses from a dying country in dire need of them. As for the nurses themselves, who would turn down such an attractive offer when the country was falling apart and all hope was gone? Who would not want to build a promising future for themselves in the States? How could I blame them?

As the days and months went by, more and more nurses resigned. Ironically, we were helping the powerful United States solve their shortage at a time when we could hardly survive. There was a ban on all foreigners, so that source was gone. And staff absenteeism remained a constant problem, with only an average of thirty percent of the nurses reporting for duty.

In the face of universal indifference the war continued and the atmosphere at the hospital worsened, affecting the morale of all. On November 21 we met with several senior staff members to discuss the various problems and evaluate the situation. The following points were mentioned: (1) patients were not looked upon as human beings; (2) medical and nursing staff were assuming an indifferent attitude; (3) no initiative; (4) time management skills needed to be improved; (5) coping with the absence of staff; (6) cultural differences between Lebanese and Philippine nurses; (7) frustration with work; (8) nurses, especially new graduates, were depressed, indifferent; (9) staff members were difficult to control; (10) lack of water, linen, housekeeping services; (11) irregularity in applying rules and regulations; (12) young nurses felt they had no time to speak to patients; (13) new graduates felt frustrated that senior nurses did not care or had no time to talk to them; (14) not enough qualified staff; and (15) paperwork was taking too much time.

We made the following recommendations: (1) to form an ad hoc committee that would meet regularly with new graduates to give them the opportunity to express their feelings and help them come to terms with the reality of nursing in a war zone (there were no social workers or psychotherapists available); (2) to meet with directors of other nursing schools and services to exchange ideas; (3) to hold a session on time management; (4) to institute group therapy; and (5) to hold in-service sessions on crisis management and coping strategies.

Since we could not rely on foreign help anymore (who would step foot in this land?), we had to deal with what we had and depend on a steady supply of creativity and ingenuity. I had several good supervisors, among them Salpi Buchakjian, who started out as a staff nurse in the Coronary Care Unit, then was promoted to head nurse and later was asked to assume the position of supervisor. She worked hard, hand in hand with her staff, to maintain standards, was always on the alert for opportunities to help others and had a wonderful sense of humor, which she so often used to defuse a problematic situation. One day she decided it was not worth staying in Lebanon and emigrated to the U.S. I miss her and so many others like her who were here during those terrible times. AUBMC could not have survived without such people.

Despite all the work, all the pressures, despite my fears and flagging spirits, I kept trying to think of ways to make a difference. I even considered the idea of opening a home health care agency for those patients who had nowhere to go. Lebanon did not have proper nursing homes. In normal times families had managed to nurse their own. But, with the disruption of war, things were no longer the same. I thought we could train professionals to take care of such patients in nursing homes rather than have them occupying hospital beds needed for those more critically ill. Such a project, I thought, would not only help AUB, but also take my mind off myself and help me grow professionally. But it was not to be. In investigating the feasibility of the project I discovered the maze of bureaucratic red tape its implementation would involve, not to mention the fact that as an American, I would not be permitted to undertake it.

The fighting continued on and off in November. That month I needed to go to the Ministry of Education—which was located near the National Museum, lying on the dividing line between East and West Beirut, the so-called Green Line where most of the fighting occurred. So, one day when it appeared to be calm, I had an AUB driver take me there. As we

The School of Nursing, still functioning despite the turmoil of war

were crossing the Green Line, from west to east, shooting broke out and before I knew it I was out of the car and ducking down and away from the rain of bullets that were falling. So this is how my life is going to end, I thought to myself, when suddenly the shooting stopped.

Towards the end of the year my morale hit its lowest point, even though my assistant director Chantal Madi did her best to support me. We worked well together, though we had our differences. Fortunately, she was one of those who chose to stay and help keep the hospital running, even though she lived on the east side and it was not easy for her to get to AUB. During Christmas I made a special effort to celebrate. I did not want the spirit of Christmas to die; all through my life it had always meant so much to me. So I arranged for my

secretary's husband to act as Santa Claus and we went off together to visit every child on the AUB campus. But then I came home and, alone again with my thoughts dwelling on the past joys of Christmas with family, I sank into deep depression. My only surcease was pill-induced sleep. I thought about suicide. Then I thought about my staff—what would they say and who would be there to take my place? It would not be right to desert them. I thought about my mother and my brothers, George and André, and how much I would miss them. Besides, it was important to keep my reputation intact and not embarrass anyone; I had a position to safeguard. I realized later that such rationalizations could hardly lead to the mad act of suicide, that the real, basic reason I did not commit suicide was because I had a very firm stake in life. I was, in essence, a survivor. I still am.

As I look back on those days I still can not understand how I lived through all the pressure. The only thing I knew was that it was important to continue to believe in the goal I had set up for myself and not to give up. Today I have scars that I can not erase, even with all the changes for the better that have occurred. I am stronger when handling problems, but also vulnerable to feelings of loneliness. There were times when I hated myself for remaining and other times when I would sit and cry for the victims of the war. Emotionally on a roller coaster, I was out of control, not being able to predict my feelings from day to day. One day I felt content and satisfied and the next I felt depressed and wanted to give up. I did not know how to handle these mood swings. I had no support system and had to rely on myself. It was different with my Lebanese friends, whose ties with family gave them a sense of security that kept them going. My family was thousands of miles away.

A lull in the fighting

## Chapter Ten
# Personal and Medical Evacuations

The year 1989 began in disappointment. My secretary, Nora Jeranian, who had been so loyal, decided to transfer to another department. She may have had her reasons, but it was a terrible blow to me. I had lost another loyal individual I had counted on. I was very hurt, but such issues ceased to affect me. It was as though I had become desensitized. Supervising the diploma program and also handling all my responsibilities as director of nursing kept me on the go. But I kept thinking of the home health care agency I had wanted to establish and was pleased when I found someone who expressed interest in the project. If I was not going to be able to do it, why not help someone else? So I gave him the material I had collected, as well as my thoughts on the subject, and wished him well.

On February 16 the fighting began again, but this time on the east side of Beirut between the Lebanese Forces, a rightist group, and the Lebanese Army. Thirty-five people died in the clashes. On the west side it remained more or less calm until March 14. As I was crossing the street from the hospital to the Emergency Unit a thunderous explosion went off in the parking lot just to my right. Glass and metal flew everywhere, but fortunately no one was severely hurt. But why was the hospital parking lot bombed? I looked at the pieces of cars lying about in the rubble and thought they could have been pieces of my body instead. Within the hour fighting heated up in West Beirut. That day we received forty-five casualties—with only fifty percent of our staff able to report for duty.

On March 16 Chief of Staff Dr. Marwan Uwaydah and his deputy, Dr. Faysal Najjar, sent the following letter to all hospital personnel:

*Amidst the growing tension and disturbing uncer-*
*tainties that have suddenly surrounded us, your*
*exemplary performance in the past and during the*
*recent painful events stands out as a vivid illustration*
*of our strong determination to continue our sacred*
*mission of caring for the sick and upholding the*
*Medical Center's tradition of excellence. The prompt*
*yet calm response to the call of duty, the meticulous*
*and efficient management of the critically injured,*
*the sympathetic attitude towards the crowd of*
*distressed and panicky relatives, all characterized*
*your conduct during those long difficult hours.*
*Indeed, you successfully shouldered an unusual bur-*
*den with a confidence and maturity that deserve our*
*highest appreciation.*

On March 24, Good Friday, the entire crossover points between East and West Beirut closed. The shelling continued day and night, east, west and north. Trying to sleep during these barrages was almost impossible. Worse

Car bomb explosion in the AUBMC parking lot

152

still were the times when I had fallen asleep and was jolted awake by the noise of the rocket launchers nearby, shooting off their deadly missiles. All Beirut was in flames. It went on for ten days. For protection, people piled up bags of sand against their windows and doors. Everywhere you went there were sandbags. Even on campus and in our building, the bags were used to shield the windows between each flight of stairs.

What had set off the new conflict was a disagreement about the presence of Syrian forces in Lebanon. General Michel Aoun, appointed commander of the Lebanese Army by President Amin Gemayel, had dared to request the Syrians to withdraw their forces from Lebanon, something no one had done before. The Syrian army had been in Lebanon since 1976, supposedly to safeguard the Lebanese and protect them from each other during the civil strife. What was General Aoun's plan for Lebanon? He wanted the Syrians out and also requested that President Bush expedite the withdrawal of Israeli forces from South Lebanon. But the U.S. chose not to interfere. As the battles raged on the number of dead and wounded mounted and the destruction of the city spread.

On March 27, as painful as it was, I had to ask the administration to close two units. Absenteeism among staff peaked and we simply did not have enough people to run the hospital. I determined that the five nurses needed to run each unit would be more useful in other more critical areas that were understaffed. From February 15 to March 31, we received 300 casualties; on March 14 alone, they numbered eighty-four. On April 7 we had to close a third unit in pediatrics and shift its staff to other more critical units.

The fighting between Aoun's Lebanese forces and the Syrian Army intensified. On the night of April 3 I heard the whoosh of shells near my apartment being launched to the east side from a Syrian tank. Then came a loud explosion. I got up and quickly dressed, expecting to run for safety any minute—but where? At two o'clock in the morning the tank moved to the front of my building. I was sure the Lebanese Army knew exactly where that tank was located and would certainly retaliate. At this point neither the Syrians nor the Lebanese cared that this was AUB, an American institution. I decided it was time to go down to the shelter we had in the basement and join all the others huddled there. One of the rockets launched from the east had just landed on the Chemistry Building, one block away from us and set fire to all the cars around it. There was no fire department, not even hoses, to put out the fire—only the sad futility of people rushing back and forth with buckets of water. AUB's deputy president, Dr. Salti, tried to get the Syrian forces to move away from the University area, but his pleas fell on deaf ears. It was not until they apparently realized their position was known to the enemy that they withdrew.

We later learned that AUB students loyal to Aoun had been conveying information to the east side on the lay-out of the University and the location of the Syrian guns. Did they not realize some of their friends and even themselves would be hurt or killed? Or maybe they did, which could be why the bombardments occurred at night instead of during the day when classes were in ses-sion. I left the basement shelter at 5:30 a.m. and returned to my apartment with one single thought in mind—to make myself a cup of strong, hot coffee. But there was no water, not a drop. This simple deprivation fell upon me like the proverbial straw on a camel's back. In another two hours I would be starting another day at the hospi-tal; my nerves were shattered. I desperately needed sleep and here I was, without even the comfort of a cup of coffee to revive my spirits.

All during the next day a barrage of shells from the east side kept falling in the area around the hospital. No longer able to tolerate the lack of sleep, I decided to spend the next night in Building 56, the nurses' dorm. But, by 10 p.m., I felt so uneasy, so displaced, that I asked an AUB driver to take me back to my apartment. Fortunately that night turned out to be a quiet one and I fell into a lovely, sound sleep that lasted until dawn.

The nursing shortage continued to be my main concern. During April my diploma students had their first day in the clinical area. I felt so proud of them in their blue uniforms, but would they get to graduate, I wondered, or would the fighting go on and on and on? On April 11, when we saw some French ships anchored offshore, we wondered why they were here and worried what would happen if the Syrians began to shell them. I had gone to get a haircut and on my way back to the hospital a rocket fell on one of the streets leading to the hospital. It had been quiet that day and I thought I could venture out in safety. How many times and how closely I missed death!

On April 13 the French Minister of Health Affairs visited the hospital. When I met him he asked if I needed anything. I told him we needed nurses, even though I knew that was just wishful thinking. Who would come to Lebanon? He offered, however, to take thirty of our patients back to France for treatment and discussed with our administrative team the choice to be made. They could not be patients intubated on mechanical respirators, but only those who could be easily transported without danger to their condition. A medical committee was formed to choose the patients. A typed discharge summary had to be sent with each one; their identification cards had to be collected or, if they had none, an official identifying paper had to be written. We had to work fast. Of course, the news quickly spread and we had all the patients clamoring to go to France. Even people who were not injured but wanted to accompany patients tried to get on the list. It was decided that only one person, preferably a woman, would be appointed to accompany the whole group.

Patients asked, "Why not me? I am injured. I want to go to France. Maybe I can stay and build a future there." They saw it as the chance of a lifetime. People were calling my office and begging me to put them on the list. Finally, the thirty were chosen and ready to go. They were to be transported to South Lebanon in ambulances from whence they would board the French ship awaiting them, a ship with a hospital facility equipped with all that was needed to care for them during the voyage. At three in the afternoon, on the day of their departure, we were given notice that the convoy would be postponed because the leader of the PSP, Walid Jumblatt, had threatened to shell any ship intending to dock. And, as if to further thwart the mission, heavy shelling resumed that day.

The shelling went on all week, always at night. During the day, while we were working non-stop at the hospital, the combatants would sleep; and at night when we were desperate for sleep, the fireworks would begin. Sometimes I would put a movie on the video to at least distract me, if not drown out the noise. On the evening of April 14 a 155-millimeter shell hit a bathroom on the fourth floor in the hospital, pierced the chemistry lab on the third floor and continued on down to the dietary department on the second floor. It was eleven o'clock in the evening and a nurse had just left the fourth-floor room after giving the patient there his medication. Electricity in the operating room suddenly went off and water pipes began leaking. The surgeons had decided to start operating in the Recovery Unit when the emergency power suddenly kicked in.

That same day shells landed on the fifth, sixth, seventh and ninth floors on the side facing East Beirut and we had to quickly move patients to the other side, though we kept having to guess which direction would be safest. Other shells fell near the AUB post office, Ada Dodge Hall, College Hall and Jafet Library. Meanwhile, although the Medical School with its 268 students continued classes, the spring recess of non-medical students was extended. Shells were falling everywhere in Beirut. Everyone was in danger. But, at the hospital, we had helpless people to care for and work went on as usual.

April 16, a Sunday, started quietly. Perhaps too quietly, like the calm before the storm. Then all hell broke loose again and, as I rushed in my car to get to the hospital, shells were falling left and right. Out of the seventy-five casualties that poured in, twelve were extremely critical. One of our medical librarians, Alice Haddad, was killed when a rocket fell at the main entrance to the library and cut her into pieces. The windows in Building 56 were all shattered, but luckily there were only a few nurses in the dorms and no one was hurt. During this attack I debated whether to move patients down to the basement but I decided against it. It was not an air raid, like in 1982, which meant that the top floors would not be as dangerous as the lower floors. I made rounds of all the units to make sure the patients were not in danger. The shelling leveled off by six in the evening. We had to add beds to accommodate the casualties. We had already stopped elective admissions to the hospital and predictions were that the patient overload would continue.

On Monday I went to work exhausted. My priority task that day was to again prepare the thirty patients for their departure to France. We had received notice that the convoy had clearance, and it was scheduled to leave the next day. With the help of the house staff I made all the

Hole in the wall caused by the bombs that hit AUBMC

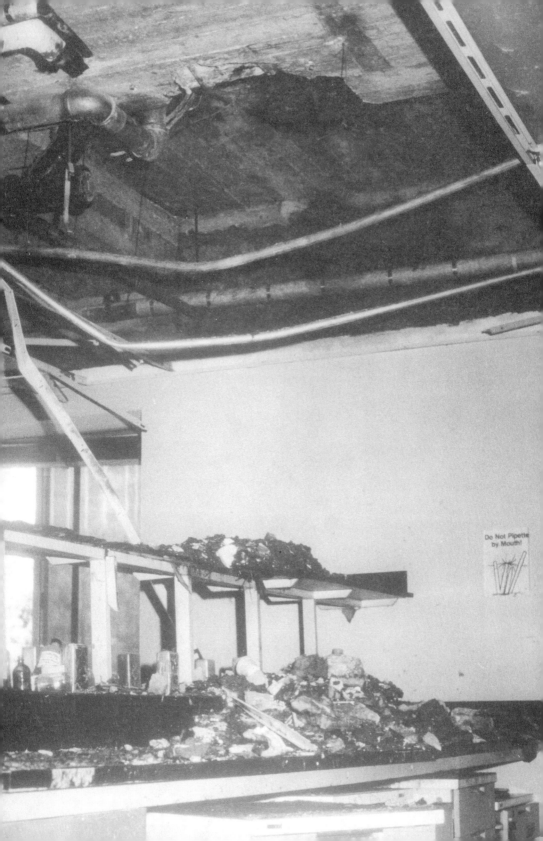

Do Not Pipette
by Mouth!

necessary preparations and went home, looking forward to taking a warm, relaxing shower and sitting on my balcony to watch the sunset. There was no hot water. The last thing I needed in my life at that moment was the shuddering splash of cold water running down my back. That evening the hospital was hit again. To all of us it was a final devastating blow to our morale. Despite the severe shortage of staff and supplies, despite the repeated damage to the hospital by shelling, despite the lack of water (cold as well as hot), we had treated at least 200 casualties during that two-week period. Many of our nurses and others had taken personal risks to report for duty. The Lebanese Red Cross had helped in securing medical supplies. The linen department had worked with the physical plant's supply of well water to provide the sheets and pillowcases and towels and uniforms we needed. Never mind that they were yellow from the brackish water; they were, at least, clean. We had to heat water, jealously gathered and stored, for the hot water baths of our burn patients.

On April 19, one day later than scheduled, the convoy set off on the first leg of its voyage to France. I was at the hospital at four in the morning to supervise the transport of the patients onto stretchers and into the vans that were waiting to take them to the port in Sidon where the French fleet was anchored. Curiously, all the shelling suddenly stopped, as though it had been programmed and someone somewhere had pressed a button. Families were there, in tears, bidding farewell to their loved ones. The French television and other media people were there recording it all for the world to watch and read about. By half-past eight, the convoy was on its way.

Almost as serious as the staff shortage were the other shortages we endured. Water, for one, and electricity for

The Chemistry lab,
destroyed by the
same bomb

another. There was absolutely no water in the areas around the hospital. True, we had our own well supply, but that needed electricity to pump out. There was no water to flush the toilets, and one of our RNs told us about voiding in a plastic bag and throwing it away. As for the shortage of leadership in the country, there was no president in Lebanon, no parliament, no cabinet. Amin Gemayel, his presidential term over, had departed for France and left the country in chaos.

On April 25 AUB Vice President George Tomey, on behalf of the president in New York, stopped by my office to thank me for my efforts. He asked me if I wanted to go to the States for a break. I thanked him and said no. I just could not imagine taking a holiday and leaving my staff and patients behind.

Following the French government's evacuation of patients for treatment in France, the Kuwaiti government offered to take a group of patients to care for them in Kuwait. For the hospital it was a welcome gesture but it was not easy to find patients ready to go to Kuwait, as most preferred to travel to the western comforts of France. Nineteen patients finally accepted to go and their transfer to Kuwait was made on May 17.

Other shortages began to plague us. Oxygen and fuel were no longer available. We had to cook the patients' food using the steam supply from our own generators, which left us with hardly enough steam to sterilize equipment. Instruments were being rendered useless by their sterilization in the brackish well water. Nevertheless, we continued to have full confidence and faith in the ultimate ability of AUB to overcome all its hardships. The institution had already survived two world wars and a number of other crises. Since it was founded, AUB had lived through many political and social transformations in Lebanon and, for many, it stood as an enduring symbol of hope. It remained a neutral entity in an irrational war. In the first five months of 1989 AUB's Medical Center had treated 719 casualties, regardless of religion or political affiliation.

On May 19 AUB President Frederic Herter sent the following tribute to all faculty, staff and students:

> *During the violence of the past two months, those of you who have selflessly safeguarded both the fabric and function of the University have been constantly in our thoughts and hearts. We salute your gallant efforts in what certainly will prove to be one of the darkest periods in AUB's long history. Special accolades must go to the medical community, students, residents, nurses, doctors and auxiliary hospital staff, who have worked so tirelessly in providing care for over 800 casualties. Those in charge of the physical plant also deserve note—never before has the campus been so violated or so quickly and effectively attended to under conditions of risk. The remarkable performance of the AUB staff under such stress is consonant with the University's long history of steadiness and resistance under fire. It gives assurance, once again, of our ability to persevere even under the most dire conditions.*

We were still in the same crisis situation when on May 12, International Nurses' Day, once again approached. On May 11 we prepared the list of patients for transport to Kuwait. We could not arrange any real celebration for Nurses' Day, but I did not want it to pass unnoticed. We sent flower arrangements to all units, distributed cookies and hung posters throughout the hospital. The next few days were quiet. Then on May 16, there was a tremendous car explosion that not

only killed its target, the Mufti Hassan Khaled, a high-ranking leader of the Sunni sect, but also killed and injured scores of people. At AUB alone, we received sixty-seven casualties, with five dead on arrival. Who did it? No one knew. The Mufti could only be identified by his clothing and ring.

The casualty count for March was 212, for April 344, and for May 337. The average overtime hours worked were 1,500 a week, with 600 a week for RNs alone. From May 14 to May 30, an average of fifty percent of the staff were absent, or a total of 175 out of 373 over a twenty-four-hour period. Moreover, there were now 186 positions in nursing services that were permanently vacant.

AUB had instituted a courier service between New York and Beirut, insuring us of regular mail deliveries, and I kept receiving letters from family and friends urging me to leave. My brother George had changed his tune and was now again pleading with me to return to the U.S.

He wrote:

*You are pressing your luck. It's only a matter of time before something happens to you.... It is stupidity to continue to stay. Leave now before it's too late...you are deteriorating emotionally and physically. I can not stand by and let you continue. You are alone, no assets, no family, and living from day to day. Get out while you can and never look back. Come here and start making a life for yourself. Every one who can leave is leaving.*

*Listen to your logic and not emotions.... You come first, not the hospital.*

Retrieving the bodies from the Mufti's car

I was sorry that George felt this way. Deep down I knew he was right, but I just could not leave. My priorities were different and I remained more determined than ever to stay.

On Wednesday, June 21, at seven in the evening, while walking on campus, I received a call on my pager from the American Embassy. It was an assistant to the ambassador, telling me that I had to leave West Beirut immediately and that an embassy car would be sent to pick me up. I was mystified by this sudden order, until I was informed that someone had threatened to kidnap me and that the directive to evacuate me had come from the State Department. When I hesitated about going, they told me they had contacted Dr. Herter and he had sent instructions that I leave immediately. I could not say no to the President of AUB, so I agreed to go the embassy on condition that I could come back the next day. I was sure it was a misunderstanding of some sort. They had never kidnapped women and I had ceased to think it might happen to me. It was getting dark, but in a matter of minutes, a big white car arrived to pick me up. It was the ambassador's bulletproof limousine. Believing I would be returning the next day, I did not pack a suitcase nor take my passport. I was not even given time to call the Dean or anyone else.

As we crossed from West to East Beirut, the embassy bodyguards kept talking continuously on a walkie-talkie. At the crossover point, we were stopped, but allowed to pass when the militiamen recognized the car and saw the embassy papers. In a way, I felt relieved to be in more or less safe hands. When we arrived at the embassy, I was received by a female officer, who escorted me to the lounge, where I met Ambassador McCarthy and another State Department official. My heart tugged with emotion to see the American flag, the Marines, the coffee percolator and all the other familiar signs of American life. It was as if I had suddenly landed in the U.S. The ambassador was extremely supportive and asked me a lot of questions about the people I worked with at the hospital and about the threats I had received.

I told the ambassador I did not want to leave, could not leave, and kept coming up with reasons why—I did not have my clothes or passport, I had not talked with the Dean about arrangements for someone to take over my duties at the hospital, I had to make sure everything would be going well there, I had to do something about my apartment, my car. But all my protests fell on deaf ears. Everyone that evening was kind and courteous. They all knew I would be leaving Lebanon the next day and tried to prepare me psychologically. I still refused to believe it would happen.

The next morning the ambassador himself informed me there was no alternative. I had to leave immediately. I would be taken by an American helicopter from Beirut to Cyprus and from there board a plane to the U.S. Everything was happening so fast, I could not think straight. I just simply went through the robot motions of what I was expected to do. I sent someone to my apartment to get my passport and a few personal items. I telephoned my office, told them I had to leave and did not know if I could ever come back. My passport had arrived, I borrowed some money and that evening at 8 o'clock, wearing a life preserver jacket, I boarded the helicopter. In Larnaca, the officer who had accompanied me from Beirut, took me to a hotel and told me he would be there the next morning to take me to the airport for my flight to New York. And that was it. I was in a daze.

On Friday, June 23, I arrived in New York at 1:35 p.m. I was now in the land of liberty and safety, away from Beirut, from the bombing, from the misery of war. But I was far from happy. That same day I went straight to the AUB office in New York to see President Herter and begged him to let me return. He told me I needed a break, a vacation, and offered me an airline ticket to Los Angeles to see my family. I went back to my hotel room, called my brothers and then went to St. Patrick's Cathedral to pray that I would see Lebanon again. All I could think about was Lebanon and AUB. Who would take care of my staff in my absence? It is true that they had an assistant director, but I kept worrying about how they were coping. My body was in New York, but my mind and heart and spirit were in Lebanon.

A few days later, the AUB office telephoned to tell me they wanted me to go to Abu Dhabi until the situation in Lebanon would allow me to return. They explained that AUB was affiliated with a government nursing school there that could very well benefit from my knowledge and experience. I was to go first to Bahrain to meet AUB's Vice President of Research and External Programs, Dr. Abdul Hamid Hallab, who would make all the necessary arrangements for my transfer to Abu Dhabi. The only comforting thought I had was that at least I would be nearer Lebanon.

On July 6, I flew to Los Angeles to see my mother and brothers. While I was there, a State Department official called to again advise me against returning to Lebanon. Dr. Herter also telephoned and told me to wait. It was wonderful to be with my family again and they did all they could to lift my spirits. I remember the drive out to Catalina Island with my brother André. It was all so peaceful and beautiful, but as he drove and I looked out at the beauty around me, all I could think of was the AUB campus.

I decided to go back to New York. I had had enough of relaxation and was anxious to know what would happen to me. When I met with Dr. Herter, he again categorically refused to let me return to Beirut and insisted that I go to the Gulf. I finally had to accept, realizing that if I ever expected to return to Beirut again, I would have to do what he wanted. He was serious. I remember him telling me at lunch one day, "Gladys, I do not want to see you in the trunk of a car. It's too risky. If you keep insisting, you will no longer have a job at AUB."

On July 15, I arrived in Larnaca, Cyprus, where I was to wait until my visa for Abu Dhabi was ready. But a week later—when Dr. Hallab contacted me and told me it would take three to six weeks before the visa would be granted—I summed up the courage to ask if I could go by boat to Lebanon and wait for my visa there in the northern part of the country, where I had friends I could stay with. That way, at least for a while, I would be in Lebanon and could get in touch with the hospital. Dr. Hallab thought about it, and being from the north himself, agreed, as long as I stayed away from Beirut. I promised.

I took the boat from Larnaca to Jounieh, where a new visa for Lebanon awaited me, and from there took a taxi to the north. I was so happy to be in Lebanon again, even though the shelling was still going on and I could see Beirut in the distance popping like firecrackers on the fourth of July. I called my office the next day and was relieved to know my department was still hanging in there and that I could help even from a distance. Beirut was in flames every night, with everyone huddled in basements, but in North Lebanon people were partying. It reminded me of Nero playing his fiddle while Rome burned.

The news, especially from West Beirut, was terrible—rockets were falling in the thousands. I kept praying that AUB would not be hit. On August 1, the kidnappers holding Joe Ciccippio threatened that at 6 p.m. they would kill him if the Shiite cleric held by the Israelis was not released. That evening, Ciccippio's execution was postponed for forty-eight hours. Seeing the picture of him on the television wrung my heart. He had a long beard and looked so very, very tired. On August 3, I heard on the radio that his execution had been postponed indefinitely. On August 8, I went down to the east side of Beirut to try to renew my residence card and work permit. It was important to do this before leaving for Abu Dhabi or else it would be difficult for me to re-enter Lebanon again. But the east side authorities were so cold and unfriendly, so full of hatred. From my papers, which had been issued in West Beirut, they knew I worked there—and there was no way they were going to help me.

The situation in Beirut, meanwhile, was getting more and more critical. By August 10, all roads to the city were closed and the electricity was cut. No one knew what would happen next. I played tennis to try to reduce the stress. And again, I tried to get my residence papers. It was not easy; your father had to be Lebanese and mine was not. Someone told me that because I had been in Lebanon for more than ten years, I was entitled to a residence permit. But that was not the case. It was hopeless. Even to this date, after more than twenty years of living in Lebanon, I have not been granted the Lebanese nationality.

I left for Abu Dhabi on August 28, feeling both excited and sad. What was waiting for me, I wondered? All I knew was that AUB had arranged that I take over nursing services at the government nursing school. The first night after my arrival, the brother of an AUB nurse took me out to dinner and to a disco. I could not remember the last time I had danced or had fun. I did not know how to anymore. And the next day, I reported to the hospital to assume my duties. Immediately, I sensed that the hospital staff felt threatened by my presence. As the days passed, they began in various small ways to make my life miserable. I must admit that I, too, bore some grudge against them, remembering that these were the people who had been recruiting nurses right from under my nose when we needed them so desperately in Beirut.

Being a nursing director in Abu Dhabi was quite different than it was at AUB. In Abu Dhabi, one could not argue with or criticize anyone. At AUBMC, we adhered to a system of policies and procedures. Here, policies and procedures took a back seat; the powers that be were always right and could dismiss you if you disagreed with them about any issues of work or personnel. How could I, who was so stubborn about principles, handle that? I had almost gotten myself killed for sticking to them. The fact that I was being paid ten times more than what I earned at AUB was not enough to make me feel any better. As the weeks passed, the frustrations continued. I was not getting along at all with the school director, who definitely did not like my being there. He just did not want me around and politely kept encouraging me to go to Kuwait or Bahrain. But stubborn Gladys was determined to stick it out.

The apartment offered to house me turned out to be unsuitable and I had arranged to stay with Lebanese friends, the Buhayris. Mr. Buhayri, then Vice President of Middle East Airlines, had left Lebanon for Abu Dhabi on a two-year leave of absence. Living with them was the only bright note during my brief stay in Abu Dhabi. They had two children and their mother Nadia was so sympathetic and caring. She herself had left Beirut reluctantly and understood the problems and turmoil I was experiencing. Without her warm, constant support, I do not think that I could have survived.

The Beirut airport finally reopened on September 4 and, soon after, Dean Mroueh telephoned to inform me that I could now return to AUB. I was ecstatic. But first, I

A boy amidst the rubble

went to Morocco to recruit nurses. I finally arrived in Beirut on October 10, back again in the hospital and work I loved. As far as the U.S. government was concerned, I was in Lebanon illegally, but I did not think twice about that risk. My staff held a welcome home party for me. My office was filled with flowers from all over the hospital and everyone toasted me with champagne. I, however, did not drink any, vowing I would not until Joe Ciccippio was released. The welcome from everyone was so warm, so sincere. It was nice to know I was wanted and needed.

I was assigned a bodyguard, who accompanied me to and from work, to the market, even on my daily walk on campus. But it got to be so claustrophobic, I could not take it anymore. It had been my decision to return, but that did not mean I had to be put in a cage. I did not want to feel like a prisoner and kept asking to be set free. But it was not until after two of the hostages, David Jacobsen and Reverend Weir, were released that I was able to convince AUB that I no longer needed a bodyguard.

The situation had calmed down and, from all indications, was expected to remain calm. In the fall of 1989, AUB received a record of 12,000 applications for admission, but only the top ten percent were accepted for the 1989-90 scholastic year. Entrance to the University was still very competitive and AUB wanted to preserve its high standards. In comparison, there had been 4,700 applicants in 1987-88 and 7,500 in 1988-89.

It was a relief to see 1989 end. In December, the president of the Nurses' Chapter of the AUB Alumni Association, Layla Farhood, had to leave for the States to finish her Ph.D. and asked me to accept the nomination as president to replace her. I was very reluctant, feeling tired and not wanting to take on any more responsibilities. I knew it would involve work and not just a title. But she and others kept after me and I finally agreed. Later, I was glad I had accepted the position. The AUB Chapter was the wealthiest alumni chapter and I was able to use it to sponsor workshops and conferences on nursing and undertake other projects to improve the image of nursing. Ours was the only chapter in Lebanon to own a nursing home, which at the time was still occupied by the Lebanese Forces. One day we will reclaim it and, with proper funds, rebuild it and realize the dream of those who initially worked to establish it.

## Chapter Eleven

# Water Supply Cut

The year 1990 was the year of water shortages. Water, water everywhere, but not a drop to drink! It all started on January 30 at three in the afternoon, when General Aoun completely cut off the municipal water supply to West Beirut. He accused the government of President Elias Hrawi of stealing money, of withholding funds from the citizens of East Beirut, and in retaliation decided to cut off the water supply. This action, of course, sparked a new round of fighting. Shells began flying across the city again, from east to west and west to east. We on the west found ourselves without water and electricity, and hence without bread. People from both sides were kidnapped and tortured. On Friday, February 1, the hospital received a total of 43 casualties, eight dead on arrival. Again, the situation became critical when the hospital began running out of water. Because of the lack of rain, the AUB wells could not supply us with enough water for our needs. Which meant we had to start rationing.

Block-long bread lines resulting from the shortage

That same day, Chief of Staff Dr. Marwan Uwaydah issued this directive:

> Because of the critical shortage of water, all elective
> admissions will be stopped, effective immediately
> and until further notice. Your close cooperation in
> minimizing water consumption in order to continue
> to provide emergency care will be greatly appreciated.

My faculty apartment building was limited to one hour of water a day. In the hospital, only cold water was available and we had to heat water by the potful in any way we could manage. We used bottled mineral water for drinking. We used distilled water from the kidney dialysis machines for sterile water. Patient discharges were expedited. Again, many staff members were unable to report to work and diploma students were asked to volunteer their services. During the month of February, a total of 1,775 casualties were brought in to the Emergency Unit, with 236 dead on arrival. On the University campus, the girls' dorm was hit and students had to move to other quarters. It was decided to expedite all patient discharges, and we went around to all the units asking those patients who could be cared for at home to leave.

My friend, Nadia Buhayri, and her two girls, who had moved back to Beirut, sought refuge with me in my campus apartment. I learned a lot from Nadia on how to handle shortages, water or otherwise. Because cooking gas was low, our whole meal was cooked in one pot and we used as few utensils as possible, even to the point of using the same coffee cup all day. We collected wastewater in pails to flush toilets and saved bath water to mop floors. The shelling, at one point on Saturday night, February 2, became so heavy that the windows of my apartment shook. Then suddenly, it was quiet; the complete eerie silence of a no-man's-land that left us no less frightened.

The next day, water was restored. We all rushed to fill pails, run the washing machine, clean the house, take showers, then fill the bathtub, wash vegetables, do our cooking, all before it disappeared again. Never mind that the water was brackish, an uninviting yellow orange in color. At the hospital, water was still a problem. There was no more distilled water, so we had to buy mineral water and add it to the oxygen flow meters. We had to connect a hose from the Kidney Unit to the Formula Room to provide soft water for the babies' formulas. And with no distilled water in the operating rooms, we could not mix the disinfectant solution to wash the nursery isollettes.

On February 15, for the very first time since the beginning of the war, we received casualties from the east side of Beirut. It was eleven o'clock at night when nineteen of them, none seriously wounded, were admitted to the Recovery Unit. They appeared to be members of the Lebanese forces who had been fighting against General Aoun and had fled to the west side escorted by the Syrians. It was a surprise to us all. They, on the other hand, were frightened. Being in "enemy territory," they feared we would harm them, perhaps try to inject them with lethal drugs. One of them asked, "Are you going to kill us?" We assured them we would take care of their injuries, feed them and make sure no one learned of their presence. They were young and many carried hashish with them. Many of our staff had relatives, fathers and brothers, who had died fighting against these people and my major concern was that they would not allow their emotions to interfere with their work. It was our duty to provide care irrespective of race, religion or political affiliation, but I prayed the militiamen would be discharged before any problems arose. The sooner they left, the better. Fortunately, nothing happened—our nurses and house staff performed and behaved admirably—and two days later, to the relief of everyone, the men were transported to the east side.

On February 18, the combatants agreed to a cease-fire and the next day the University reopened and resumed classes. But the lack of water, with all its accompanying problems, persisted. The hospital required 300,000 liters of clean water a day to produce enough distilled water for its needs. This shortage was especially severe in the preparation of disinfectant solutions and we had to depend on the Chemistry Department to supplement our distilled water supply. It may not be considered important, but because every drop counted, we discontinued the circumcision of male newborns.

By the end of February we had taken care of 161 casualties, and not until the middle of March did the water shortage ease. On Sunday, March 18, we even had hot water. I had been using bottled water heated on the stove to wash my hair, and showers, always cold, were few and far between. At the hospital, we had been getting burn cases resulting from people heating water in pots, yet we hardly had enough water to treat those cases with a tub bath. Imagine that in an age of computers and advanced technology one could still revel in and give thanks for one of the basic necessities of life.

On April 31, hostage Frank Reed was released and we

Waiting in line for water due to the severe shortage

all prayed that Joe Cicippio and Tom Sutherland, our AUB people, would be next. That day, the hospital was without electricity for more than two hours. The operating rooms had to shut down. The entire hospital lay in darkness. The dumbwaiters were out, which meant we could not send food trays to the patients. So we decided on sandwiches, which we piled on trays and carried from one floor to the next up to the tenth, with flashlights lighting our way, to reach every one of the almost 400 patients waiting to be fed. As exhausting as the work of continuously ambu-bagging the patients on respirators was, it was done for more than two hours in order to keep them breathing and alive.

Heavy shelling recommenced on May 9. As a result, plans for celebrating International Nurses' Day on 12 May had to be modified once again. Nevertheless, through the Nurses' Chapter, I was able to organize a Health Promotion Day, at least to keep the image of nursing alive in the public's eye.

In June, I left for The Hague, Netherlands, to speak before the Fifth European Congress on Intensive Care Medicine being held there. The topic was current issues in ICU nursing. One of those who had been impressed by my address in Montreal two years earlier had proposed to the Congress that I be invited to talk about my experiences of nursing in wartime Lebanon. I realized again how little people around the world knew about what we had been living through. They asked many questions about the coping mechanisms and strategies that we used in order to function and survive. I wished that I had some videos to show them.

Back in Lebanon, AUB held its graduation ceremonies on the Green Field for the first time since 1980. For everyone, holding commencement outdoors again was indeed a hopeful sign. Even with strict security enforced, a crowd of 5,000 people gathered to watch the 968 graduates receive their diplomas in the presence of the President of Lebanon Elias Hrawi. Years later, many Lebanese would remember that joyous day of August 14, 1990. The University had survived against all odds. Many of the faculty had left; foreign student enrollment had fallen from fifty percent to ten percent; it had been bombed and its members kidnapped; its funds depleted and its water cut off. Yet it had survived. Among those in cap and gown were the BSN graduates. As president of the Nurses' Chapter, I organized a reception for them and in my congratulatory message spoke of their future role in nursing, emphasizing the need for them to remain and work in Lebanon. They seemed so enthusiastic and committed, but I knew that many would eventually leave to follow better opportunities elsewhere.

In his address on behalf of the AUB Board of Trustees, Ali Ghandour lauded the triumph of spirit that kept AUB alive. He spoke of the "profiles of courage" that "rose above the pettiness that permeated the nation at various levels, offered guidance and direction, and undertook to help the wounds of strife and division. In essence, AUB sustained hope when lesser people despaired." He ended his address with this parable of faith:

> *And finally, on a more hopeful note, I commend to you the story of the snail climbing up a tree. He meets the woodpecker, whereupon the woodpecker asks the snail where it is heading. 'I am going up the tree to eat those beautiful green leaves at the top,' the snail answers. To which the woodpecker retorts, 'But there are no green leaves at the top of the tree.' 'There will be,' the snail answers, 'by the time I get there.' Ladies and gentlemen, we must all begin now; collectively we are duty-bound to do so, to rebuild and reshape the new Lebanon.*

The summer passed more or less peacefully. Fifteen years of civil war had taken the best years of our lives. Militia types who could not even write their names were driving brand new Mercedes cars or Range Rovers, while we professionals had to scrape to make ends meet. They made money in so many different ways—by stealing electricity from AUB and other places by rerouting and reconnecting lines, then selling power to neighborhood households for $100 a month; by rerouting telephone lines for a fee; by smuggling and drug trafficking;

by thieving in any way they could, whether privately or through embezzling government funds. The government had expanded and now included a number of militia leaders. Nevertheless, the mood in Lebanon was one of relief. In Beirut, shops began to reopen. The yacht club of the legendary Saint Georges Hotel, which was now no more than a shell of walls, began expanding its marina.

On October 13, General Aoun surrendered, requested his army to report to the new commander appointed by the President, then secretly left for France under the protection of the French government. People finally climbed out of their shelters. By early November, a cabinet was being formed and the value of the Lebanese pound (livre) had improved. The country, however, was in a shambles. The entire infrastructure of the country had been destroyed. The rebuilding of Beirut after fifteen years of devastation would need billions of dollars, plus will, patience and hard work.

In her November 1990 article in *The Washington Report on Middle East Affairs*, Elaine Larwood wrote:

*The American University of Beirut, the oldest American institution in the Middle East, is in trouble. Like Lebanon itself, mention of AUB usually gives pause. Beirut? American? How could any institution, particularly American, survive in Beirut? But survive it does and with a good deal of courage and practice, plus a measure of necessary compromise. Balancing problems against potential, the University's administration has concluded that AUB is somewhere 'beyond survival.'*

*'We are working on the premise that a University
that is 124 years old cannot simply succumb to
stagnation and inactivity because of a mere
$8 million deficit,' AUB's Deputy President
Dr. Ibrahim Salti declared recently.*

*Founded by American missionaries in 1866,
the Syrian Protestant College, as AUB was then
known, advocated freedom of thought that
allowed the individual to choose his religion,
politics and way of life. Such ideas, new to the
Middle East, attracted the nucleus of intellectuals
and activists who later became catalysts of the
Arab nationalist movement.*

Larwood went on to say that AUB badly needs
more money to shore up its program, attract more
qualified faculty and improve its facilities. She ends by
saying, "Whatever the forthcoming political and economic scenario, however, the American University of
Beirut's many friends look at its long history, its beautiful campus and its positive influence and think it's
worth saving."

In November, the hospital was again without water.
Pre-operative patients, with the exception of heart surgery cases, could not be bathed. We carried buckets of
water from the Kidney Unit and the Nursery, the only
units the Physical Plant provided with water. No tea or
coffee was distributed. The well water was salty and we
had to buy mineral water for essentials. Because of the
high demand, the price doubled and whisky had
become cheaper than water. As usual, the Lebanese
were clever at taking advantage of a situation. By the
middle of the month, we were still without municipal

Medical gate in the late 19th century

water. The operating suites remained closed and there was no water to flush toilets. Finally, administration contacts with the Ministry assured us of water delivery, somewhat rationed but at least coming in. Finally, it appeared, a government was in control of the country. A further good sign was that on November 18, the government announced that all militia offices would be closed and all armaments collected. Could this be possible, we wondered? Were we really finally going to have peace?

During the month of November, something strange happened at the hospital. We had an orderly named Samir who had been with us all through the war. Always a perfect gentleman, polite and neatly dressed, he was engaged to a student nurse. Always when there was trouble in the south, he would be inexplicably absent from work. When he would return, he was always very apologetic, saying he had got stuck somewhere for some reason or other and just could not make it to the hospital. I could not rely on him, but I could not terminate him. Except for his absenteeism, he was a good worker and the patients liked him. So, like so many others, he came and went as he pleased. On November 20, during one of his absences, we were informed that Samir had been killed in the south during a Lebanese commando skirmish with Israeli soldiers. It was only then that we learned that he had actually been an officer in the PLO! He had been with us for fifteen years. He had bathed patients, fed them, put them on bedpans, and none of us ever knew about his secret life. It was a shock to all, especially to me. I wondered how many more Samirs we had around the hospital. Samir was honored as a martyr and his picture was posted everywhere.

While 1990 brought us solid hope of peace and stability, the hospital continued struggling to cover its bare essentials. It was time to rebuild Lebanon, but few remained to help in its rebuilding. It required money, planning and a new influx of manpower.

## Chapter Twelve

# A Productive Year

For me, 1991 turned out to be the most stable and productive year, professionally and emotionally. One of my dreams came true when the first class of diploma nursing students, twelve in all, graduated. I had started the program during one of the worst periods of the war, and now I could see the gratifying results. Hard work and persistence, aided by my staff and University officials, had paid off. It was not easy to begin from scratch and create a health professional from individuals born of war. This program continues to graduate nurses to help meet the needs of the hospital.

With peace, we could now concentrate on activities other than survival and saving lives. I worked on a television documentary, to be shown on International Nurses' Day, that would improve the image of nursing in Lebanon and, we hoped, encourage more students to go into the profession. The documentary described the role of the nurse at AUBMC and the importance of her significance as a member of the hospital's medical care team. We also

The bombing of AUB's
College Hall

**187**

held another educational health fair. There was so much to do now after fifteen years of fighting and bloodshed. It was time now to compensate for the brain drain and rectify deficiencies. But it would not be easy. People had changed, had adopted a pattern of survival and the self-interest that usually goes with it. They did not care about national development. The economic situation did not help. Though the war filled the pockets of many, many others, who had lived comfortable lives before the war, were left destitute.

Lara Marlowe, in the July 22 issue of *Time* magazine, wrote:

> *Charles Mandini left home at age 15 to fight*
> *Palestinians in Beirut. That was in 1975.*
> *During the next 15 years, he participated in*
> *every campaign waged by the Christian Phalange*
> *militia against Palestinians, Druze, Shiite*
> *Muslims, Syrians, even other Lebanese Christians.*
> *Along the way, he lost his left eye, his spleen, a*
> *kidney, and one finger.*

Was it worth it? All over Lebanon, men and women who had survived the ferocious fifteen-year civil war were asking themselves that question. "We all lost," says Ghassan Matar, a magazine editor whose only child, a seventeen-year-old daughter, was killed by a car bomb in 1989. "How can any one say anybody won when 150,000 people died, 200,000 were wounded, and half a million left the country?"

Fortunately for AUB, our supporters in the U.S. were determined to restore the University to its former excellence. Those responsible in Beirut had the same determination. The job now was to erase the negative image left in people's minds about the standards of the University and its hospital. We had to get AUB back on its feet and repair the damages of war, physically, institutionally and intellectually.

The year would bring another war, though not in Lebanon. This one would pit Iraq against Kuwait. How could we relax when the makers of war were busy elsewhere and causing waves of repercussion throughout the region? On January 18, Hezbullah in Sidon and the Bekaa began demonstrating and went on strike, threatening to target any American institution in Lebanon. We kept our disaster plans ready and held regular refresher sessions, never knowing when we would have to mobilize them again.

On the morning of August 2, I awoke to hear that Iraq had invaded Kuwait. The first thought that came into many minds here, including mine, was that at least this war would be in someone else's back yard. But when the U.S. intervened and began sending its troops into the Gulf area, we feared the war would spread to Lebanon. I had mixed feelings. I worried that my brother George, who was a colonel in the U.S. Army Reserves, would be called up. People, even some of my friends, spoke harshly of America's involvement and I began to feel uneasy, out of place. Would they accept me as a person or would I once more experience the fear of being an American in the wrong place at the wrong time?

Having barely emerged from their own war, many people in Lebanon reverted to a survival mode of behavior. The Ministry of Health distributed literature and arranged sessions all over Lebanon, especially in the south, on how to protect one's self in the event of chemical warfare. People started buying gas masks. At AUB, we also took our precautions. The University held a seminar on chemical agents. Nursing Services also held a session on the management of mass casualties and violent injuries, addressing topics such as lung-damaging agents, their recognition and clinical effects. On the other hand, despite the disturbing repercussions of the Gulf war, there were many who did not care what was happening as long as it was not in Lebanon.

In general, life was improving. At AUB, we were full of enthusiasm as we began working out plans to get the University back to what it was before the war. Some tourists and businessmen were coming to Lebanon. Expatriates were reuniting with their families after years of separation. Beaches were crowded with people. The real estate market was booming. Western airlines began resuming flights to Beirut. The Lebanese livre was getting stronger. On the other hand, there were the problems of those displaced by the war, as well as problems with housing and unemployment. What was to be done with all the militiamen now retired from "active duty"? Even the hospital started getting applications from militiamen looking for jobs as orderlies. Could we take such people? It was true the fighting had ended, but was Lebanon's war really over?

If the war was over, certainly its effects on the people were not. In an interview with Marilyn Rashka of the *Los Angeles Times*, Dr. Hisham Baroudy, director of the AUBMC division of rehabilitation, estimated the number of handicapped in the tens of thousands. "The worst cases," he said, "are those who lost both arms and are blind. With no institutions to take care of them, they are totally dependent on their families. An artificial limb costs $1,000 or ten times the monthly minimum wage."

Ziad Kaj, an AUBMC Nursing Services clerk who writes for *Monday Morning*, a Lebanese English language weekly, tells the story of Ahmad Seifeddine, a ten-year-old boy whose leg was amputated above the knee. Confined to a wheelchair at the hospital for six months, his only wish was to walk again. He had been severely wounded in a car bomb explosion in December 1990. His aunt was killed instantly and his mother and sister were injured. Ahmad needed a nerve implantation for his right leg and a prosthesis for his left. But for technical reasons, this treatment could not be undertaken in Lebanon, and if the right leg were not operated on, it would have to be amputated as well. His father contacted many philanthropic organizations, but received nothing but sympathetic words. We never knew what happened to Ahmed, whether his father was able to find the money for the surgery and prosthesis.

On July 23, AUB's Green Field was again transformed into one vast auditorium when over 5,000 people gathered to watch 1,192 students receive their degrees. It was the second year the graduation ceremony was held outdoors and it made us feel that normal academic life had really returned for good. It was also an occasion to celebrate the 125th anniversary of the founding of AUB, a very auspicious milestone in the University's history. At the medical graduation ceremony, held a week earlier, ninety physicians and thirty-four BS nurses received their degrees from the Faculty of Medicine. I could not hold back my tears when my twelve diploma students took the Nightingale oath. These young women had come from very poor backgrounds and hardly knew anything outside their life of social, educational and cultural deprivation. We had molded them not only into nurses, but also into individuals prepared to take on the world. But first, they would help fill in the gap left by so many departing nurses. All our hard work was paying off.

Before graduation, I had gone to Sofia, Bulgaria, to recruit nurses. Because it was a poor country, I expected to find some there who would come to AUBMC for a salary of $250 a month. I managed to recruit five nurses, but when they arrived in Beirut, four of them changed their minds and insisted on returning to Bulgaria. We had no choice but to send them back.

On November 8, I was awakened from a sound sleep by a tremendous explosion. Oh God, I prayed, please, not again. Shivering, frightened and cold, I began muttering to myself as I got dressed, "I can not take it. It's too much. If it all starts again, I'm leaving this time." My first thought was to go to the Emergency Unit, but first I telephoned AUB Security to find out what had happened. They told me that College Hall had been bombed, but they did not know if there were any casualties. I went up to College Hall with George Sayegh, the Assistant Vice President, who lived in the same building as I did. I will never forget the sight that greeted our eyes. Students, Internal Security, Squad 16, and Syrian soldiers were crowded around what was left of the building. It had been reduced to rubble, the smoke still dense and the smell of leaking gas dangerously strong. Among the rubble lay the College Hall clock, the soaring timepiece that for 117 years had been tolling the hours for all of Ras Beirut. Everyone was in shock. It was thought that the building was empty. Unfortunately, one person was inside and was killed.

We telephoned President Herter in New York, where he was attending a fund-raising reception to commemorate AUB's 125th anniversary and where Mrs. Mona Hrawi, Lebanon's First Lady, was guest of honor. What terrible news to receive at an anniversary celebration. Surely the perpetrators must have planned it this way. We

The reopening of College Hall in June 1999

learned later that a van carrying the bomb, which was timed to explode during the night, had been driven onto the campus and parked in front of College Hall.

Classes were cancelled until Monday. On Saturday, work began on repairing the nearby Assembly Hall, which had been damaged in the blast. Students were helping collect its stones, piling them one on top of the other for replacement. New windows were installed. As for College Hall, it was totally destroyed. It would take three years and ten million dollars to rebuild it. The public outcry was overwhelming, as was the determination to make sure that College Hall, the symbol of AUB, would be rebuilt. Everyone united in anger against this terrible attack on the University, which for 125 years had been serving not only Lebanon but the entire region as well. In Lebanon, the community, the faculty, the staff and the students, all immediately began collecting money for the rebuilding fund. Rich and poor, even high school students, dug into their pockets. And abroad, the campaign to raise the millions needed found generous response among institutions, philanthropists and AUB alumni. The United States government, for one, pledged three million dollars. The tower clock is now in place and in 1999, the new College Hall, rebuilt as an architectural replica of the old, will open its doors.

In the meantime, happier things were happening. The hostages, one by one, were being released. Finally, to my great relief, it was Joe Ciccippio's turn. It was as though I also had been in prison and had now been freed. I could now drink that glass of champagne. By the end of the year, all the hostages had been released. It was a good feeling. During my Christmas gathering for the head nurses and supervisors, I told them three of my dreams had come true: the hostages had been released, the diploma students had graduated, and the hospital and Lebanon were on the road to recovery.

At the hospital, we were working to reestablish our old pre-war standards. It would not be easy. For a long time, rules and regulations had been bent to accommodate the circumstances of war. Many of the staff were burned out and were dealing with economic hardships, some even lacked money to buy food. They were no longer motivated to care about standards and had little faith in Lebanon's future. With so many nurses having left Lebanon, the few that were left had no role models to strengthen their resolve.

In an effort to alleviate the nursing shortage, I went to the Philippines on a recruiting mission in December. Salaries at AUBMC were now equivalent to almost $300 a month, so surely I could find some who would take the offer. I recruited fifteen nurses, all of whom fulfilled their two-year contracts. As for me, I felt enormous satisfaction in having remained to see Lebanon begin to rise from the ashes.

## Chapter Thirteen
# 1992-1998: Aftermath, Recognition, and Change

Lebanon's key issue in 1992 was the economy. The government failed to control inflation and people, left and right, were demanding reforms and threatening to go on strike. On May 6, protesters marched in the streets in angry demonstration—which brought ten casualties to our Emergency Unit. Rocks were hurled at business establishments, especially those that traded in U.S. dollars. Everyone was carrying dollars instead of Lebanese livres. The rich were getting richer and the poor were getting poorer. Values and principles had disappeared. People were only concerned about money. And the Gulf countries were still recruiting our nurses. To see the advertisements in Beirut newspapers offering nursing jobs in Abu Dhabi and Saudi Arabia was all we needed.

On May 7, for the first time in seventeen years, the Middle East Medical Assembly was held in Beirut, with President Elias Hrawi present at the opening ceremony. For

The release of David Jacobsen (second from left), with my brother (right) and his wife (left)

all of us, it was an exciting event. It meant that we were regaining our regional stature in the medical field. Around twenty physicians—seventy-five percent of them AUB graduates—were invited to present papers. All of them were Lebanese who had achieved prominence in medicine around the world and, as such, could contribute significantly to the profession in Lebanon. The organizers of the assembly did a superb job. In addition to bringing together an outstanding roster of speakers, they put on an impressive exhibition of the latest in medical supplies and equipment. In his speech, President Hrawi saluted AUB's long record of excellence and paid special tribute to the freedom of expression that distinguished the University among all others in the region.

On International Nurses' Day, May 12, the AUB Nurses' Chapter organized a conference on the theme, "Promoting

The release of Joe Ciccipio (head of table)

the Image of the Professional Nurse." The keynote speaker was Dr. Huda Abou Saad, a Lebanese living in the Netherlands, who spoke on trends in nursing research. AUB President, Dr. Herter, who sent his greetings on the occasion, had this to say about our nurses:

> *The nursing profession had a critical and largely unsung importance in keeping AUB alive over the past century, particularly during periods of conflict. For many Lebanese, the AUBMC is the core of the University; the fact that our doctors and nurses and paraprofessionals provided unceasing aid to all elements of the community without discrimination and during the worst of the violence, insured the safety and integrity of AUB as a whole. And in times of peace, our Nursing School has played a preemi-*

*nent role in education, just as our loyal cadre of nurses in AUBMC, under the leadership of Ms. Mouro, has served as a model for dedicated patient care in the community. This is a distinguished lega- cy to carry into the next century.*

As president of the Nurses' Chapter, I received other congratulatory messages that week. Understanding that recognition is basic to motivation, I shared them all with my nurses. Carol Boston, Executive Director of the American Organization of Nurse Executives, wrote:

*It has been brought to my attention by Joseph J. Ciccippio that you have been Director of Nursing at the American University Medical Center in Beirut for the past seventeen years! I would like to take this opportunity to recognize you and your nursing staff for your commitment and dedication to the nursing profession.*

*As nurses in the United States, we recognize that you and your nursing staff have surpassed insur- mountable conditions. You not only struggled with the rapid changes in health and its effect upon the nursing profession, but faced the impossibilities and devastations of war on a daily basis. It is a pleasure to commend your dedication and commitment to the profession.*

Lucille A. Joel, President of the American Nurses Association, wrote:

*On behalf of the members of the American Nurses Association, I am writing to extend to you and your*

*nurse colleagues greetings and best wishes for*
*Nurses' Day. As we celebrate Nurses' Day across the*
*United States and internationally, we are reminded*
*of the many courageous and caring acts by nurses*
*for the world's citizens. The nurses of Lebanon have*
*faced particular challenges across the years. For this,*
*you have our admiration and gratitude.*

AUB was well into normal activities again, with its various faculties putting on exhibitions, concerts and plays and organizing lectures and seminars. As for the hospital, we were moving full speed ahead. Two units had been remodeled, the operational framework was better organized, and long-range planning was underway.

Again, for the third year in a row, graduation ceremonies took place on the Green Field. There were 926 graduates. AUB also celebrated the opening of the Hariri Faculty Apartments, a ten-story building that includes twenty, two-bedroom and ten, three-bedroom apartments. It was donated by Mr. Rafic Hariri, a billionaire of Lebanese birth and a philanthropist of the first order. Through the war years, he had provided thousands of scholarships to Lebanese university students, both at home and abroad. As a gesture of recognition and appreciation, AUB asked Mr. Hariri to give the commencement address. I, in turn, was gratified by the graduation of our second class of diploma nursing students. There were now twenty-one more new nurses to fill the gap in our ranks.

November 8 saw the laying of the cornerstone of College Hall by President Hrawi, launching its reconstruction and signaling a promising future for AUB and for Lebanon. As the President remarked that day, "The war in Lebanon has ended, but the war for Lebanon has not."

In January 1993, Deputy President Dr. Ibrahim Salti,

who for six years had given his best to AUB in the worst possible circumstances, resigned. He was replaced by Dr. Samir Makdisi, an AUB professor of economics and former minister of economy in the Lebanese government. In June, Dr. Herter resigned as president of AUB and Dr. Robert Haddad was appointed in his place. All was safe and secure again, no shelling, no shooting, and no kidnapping. Gradually, some of our faculty began returning.

As for developments on a national level in 1993, Rafic Hariri was appointed prime minister, a new cabinet was formed and parliamentary elections were held, giving everyone hope that the country was truly on the road to recovery. The Lebanese currency stabilized, more and more shops reopened, many new buildings started going up, and work began on the vast reconstruction of Beirut's central district, which had been totally devastated during the war. It was good to see this progress. But the cosmetics of rebuilding and reinstituting law and order would not be enough to bring back the values and principles needed to mend the deeply damaged fabric of Lebanon's society. This was where the real reconstruction had to begin, within the spirit of the people themselves.

We also could not ignore the Israeli occupation of Lebanon in the south and the continuing threat of danger it posed to the country as a whole. Toward the end of July, one of our practical nurses, Ali Murtada went on a suicide mission against Israel in the south. He was a member of Hezbullah and had left a farewell message with a photograph of himself to be circulated throughout the hospital. Still young, with a wife and two small children, he was a quiet man who prayed often and kept trying to convince those around him to convert to Islam. We had no idea he was so passionately involved in religion and politics. I had had some problems with him through the years, but we always more or less came to terms on certain issues. For example, because of his religious affiliation, he insisted on growing a beard, which was against staff regulations. It took a while to convince him, but he finally shaved it off.

His death saddened me. I attended a memorial service held for him by Hezbullah at AUB's West Hall. It was an experience I will never forget. I was one of the very few women present wearing a skirt and not a *chador*, the long black dress that covers a woman's entire body from head to toe. The Shiite sheik who conducted the ceremony talked about Ali as a martyr who had given his life in the service of God and was now living in a better world. He also attacked the U.S. and Americans for their pro-Israeli policies. This went on for an hour and a half. I could hardly breathe. I gave my condolences and left the hall in relief.

A week after Ali died, Hezbullah renewed its attacks against Israel and by the end of July, the entire region of the south, from the sea to the Bekaa Valley, where Hezbullah was headquartered, was in turmoil. Israel warned the people to leave the area, then retaliated with a full-scale barrage of rockets, one after another, completely demolishing their homes. The south became a no man's land, as almost 300,000 people fled the area and came to Beirut. The Israelis were determined to destroy Hezbullah, but who suffered? The innocent, the children, the old, and the helpless. I felt as though we were reliving the Israeli invasion of 1982. Everyone feared the shelling would extend to Hezbullah locations in Beirut, which would be catastrophic. At the hospital, we hurriedly prepared ourselves. Most of those experienced in disaster management had left, leaving only the head nurse, myself and a couple of supervisors with knowledge in handling mass casualty situations. We formed a new disaster team, reviewed our supply needs and outlined our revised disaster plan with the physicians and all others concerned with Emergency Unit procedures.

The mother of one of our gate men was killed in the south. My secretary, Lina, had twenty refugees, with no other place to go, staying in her home in Beirut. In one week, we received around fifty casualties, among them burn cases as in 1982. The bodies of an entire family that had perished in the ruins of their home were brought in to be kept in our morgue. Many of our support personnel were from the south and worry over their families made it difficult for them to focus on their work. AUB students were collecting money, supplies and food to care for the mass of refugees. The U.S. requested an end to the fighting; the Arab League met in Syria on July 31; and finally, on August 1, all hostilities ceased.

On October 7, professors, staff and students crowded into the Assembly Hall for the opening ceremonies of the 1993-94 academic year. A message from AUB President Dr. Robert Haddad called on students to use the knowledge gained in their undergraduate years in a rational way. He urged them to avoid overspecialization and expose themselves instead to a wide variety of disciplines, saying that specialization should be left to graduate studies.

On October 19, the Office of Nursing Services honored Matilda Abboud, associate director of Nursing Services, who retired after devoting twenty-seven years of her life to AUB. She had been head of the Practical Nurse Training Program, which began under her leadership in 1966 and, since then, has graduated 614 practical nurses. The year 1993 also saw the third class of diploma nursing students graduate. The program had now produced a total of sixty-five nurses. I continued to feel proud.

The year 1994 was a special year for me personally. The AUBMC director, Dr. Faysal Najjar, and the medical dean, Dr. Adnan Mroueh, resigned and were replaced by

Dr. Raif Nassif and Dr. Samir Najjar respectively. These changes, though expected, caused much anxiety among the staff, including me. Such changes always create apprehension, but through the years I had come to realize that changes in administration could not change my commitment and dedication to the institution I loved.

At times, I regretted the day I came to AUB. I had experienced many frustrations in trying to change attitudes and instill the values, principles and standards of behavior I believed in. So often I had wanted to quit, but then I would wake up the next day with a renewed energy that came from heaven knows where and I would say to myself, "Do not give up, Gladys Mouro. You cannot let AUB down." Now, we who had stuck it out and survived throughout the war are exhausted, but our loyalty to AUB remains undiminished. However, we need the input of new human energies, new ideas and resources to support us in rebuilding for the future—a future guided by the lofty principles of AUB's founders.

On May 7, His Excellency Marwan Hamade, Minister of Health, awarded me Lebanon's Silver Order of Health. It was presented to me at a Nurses' Day dinner attended by over 500 people. I also received awards of appreciation from the Ministry of Health, both personally and on behalf of the Office of Nursing Services, as well as one from the health sectors of Arab countries. Four other nurses also received awards of appreciation from the Ministry of Health for their long periods of service.

I was surprised and gratified to have been recognized by the Lebanese government. It was a day to remember. I only wished my family could have been there on this memorable occasion. After dinner, there were speeches, a performance of folklore dancing, and a cake in the shape of Florence Nightingale's lamp was cut. My nurses, along with the entire AUBMC medical staff, were all there beaming with pride. The University of Pennsylvania, where I received my master's degree, recorded the event in its alumni newsletter.

On May 13 the 29th Middle East Medical Assembly was held in Beirut, again under the auspices of President Elias Hrawi, and that summer another class of graduates donned their caps and gowns to receive their diplomas on the Green Field. At the University, things were going well until the administration announced a ten percent increase in tuition fees for the coming year. On October 10, the students protested by calling a strike, in which clashes occurred between government security forces and the strikers. It was 1973 all over again. That evening, the hospital received twenty-two casualties. Fortunately, the strike did not last long and classes soon resumed.

Just a week before I had received a letter from my mother berating me for continuing to remain in Beirut. She thought it was crazy, beyond reason, how I continued to throw my life away. "What you're making there," she wrote, "is nothing at your age. One of your nurses that you trained earns $5,000 a month, a simple nurse....Do what you want....We are not going to kill ourselves trying to convince you. You can live there in the dark." I felt sad and confused. Logic said she was right. Why do I stay? It is hard to make her understand why when I do not understand it myself. Is it the satisfaction of giving and knowing that my giving might make a difference? Is it because I gave so much and did not want to see my efforts go down the drain? If the value system I believe in so much and have tried to restore never returns, then my mother and the others who advised me years and years ago to leave would be right. Yet, because of my faith in AUB and Lebanon, I cannot see or accept that.

The war is over, but we are battling hatred, anger,

resentment, selfishness, and the lack of loyalty and sense of belonging. Is it because of the economic pressures? Is it the psychological damage of war? Or is it just how people are? How can you make them honest, conscientious and disciplined, how can you instill a spirit of teamwork based on loyalty and belonging? I do not want to feel negative. It is important, as the head of a staff depending on my guidance, that I project a positive image. We must hope for the best. We simply have no other choice. The challenge ahead of us in restoring basic values is much more complex than the simple act of surviving.

Though change has not been easy after two decades of war and turbulence, the past four years have been fruitful. Standards are being rigidly adhered to and compliance is stressed. No longer is it simply a matter of surviving as an institution. We are also faced now with many new technological challenges. It was as though we had been in a twenty-year Rip Van Winkle sleep and had suddenly awakened in another world. The health care system had evolved tremendously. New medical equipment, new "tools of the trade," had been introduced. And computers had taken over. It was difficult for those in responsible positions to adjust and cope with these changes. After so many years of isolation, I found myself lost, yet it was expected of me to create an environment of adaptability that could ease the path for those around me and erase their general feelings of insecurity. Fortunately, they were used to me and had confidence that I would do all I could to help them during this transitional period.

Once the ban on American travel to Lebanon was lifted, foreigners began flocking into Lebanon, bringing with them a welcome cultural diversity. For so long we had been living in isolation, with not much more than war and survival as topics of conversation. Overnight, the country was exposed to an influx of development. Money poured in and construction quickened its pace. The new Lebanon was on its way. For some people, to whom money was the name of the game, it was an economic bonanza. But the majority of Lebanese had to tighten their belts. The middle class, once the bulwark of the nation, was disappearing; inflation began soaring and salaries were hardly enough to make ends meet.

At AUBMC, more nurses slowly but surely began leaving the hospital, this time not out of fear but for economic reasons. We were admitting a large number of patients, many of them critical cases because they had not been able to afford hospitalization early enough. As the admissions continued to increase, we were confronted once again with a nursing shortage.

In April 1996, a sudden horrible disaster occurred in the south. Israel attacked the village of Qana, a supposedly "protected" area where the U.N. forces were based. One of their bombs hit a building where hundreds of villagers had sought shelter, instantly killing 111 Lebanese, most of them women and children, and wounding 120 others. The entire country was paralyzed in shock, fearing there would be more to come. Again, many people fled the south and poured into Beirut. At AUBMC, we received a total of 350 wounded and traumatized refugees. Once again, AUB demonstrated its humanitarian capacities. I was proud, and still am, to be part of this great institution. In the face of overwhelming international censure, the Israeli military attack quickly came to a halt.

The remainder of 1996 and the years since then have been relatively peaceful, though skirmishes of varying intensity between Hezbullah and Israel continue in the south. On 13 June 1996, AUB held a memorial service for Dr. Raja Khoury. A fine, remarkable person, his death rep-

resented a great loss to AUB. He was the one who had recognized my potentials and promoted me to the position of
Director of Nursing Services.

In May, we celebrated International Nurses' Day in a
mood of stability, peace and hope. On July 17,
commencement exercises were held once again on the
Green Field; and for the first time in thirteen years, an AUB
president was on hand for the graduation. Dr. Robert
Haddad flew in from New York to spend a few weeks at the
University. In his commencement address, Dr. Haddad
paid tribute to all those who had held the fort and "who
bore AUB's burden through some sixteen years of war in
Lebanon….that the University endured this season of rage
can be attributed only to the courage and dedication of the
various elements of the AUB community….who saw to it
that AUB, like Lebanon itself, though gravely wounded,
would not die."

In September 1996, Hospital Director Dr. Raif Nassif
retired. In his place, Mr. Dieter Kuntz, a Canadian, was
appointed director. In July 1997, it was announced that Dr.
John Waterbury would replace Dr. Haddad as president of
AUB. Since the ban on American travel had been removed,
Dr. Waterbury would be taking up permanent residence in
Beirut, in Marquand House on the AUB campus. It was
marvelous to hear this. The presence of the AUB president,
an American, in Lebanon was a sure sign that stability had
returned for good. In October, Dr. Waterbury came on a
four-day visit, then returned in January 1998 to assume his
responsibilities as the first resident president of AUB in
twelve years.

Though Lebanon was returning to normal, we continued to experience scares of one kind or another. While Dr.
Waterbury was here on his four-day visit, two sticks of
dynamite were lobbed on to the AUB campus at midnight

from a speeding car. They landed on a parked car and exploded, completely destroying the car and shattering the windows of two faculty buildings. Thank God no one was injured. It was the first serious attack on AUB since the 1991 bombing of College Hall. What did this mean? Was it intended to scare away Americans, including Dr. Waterbury? Well, it did not succeed. Dr. Waterbury arrived in Beirut as scheduled and moved into Marquand House, sending out a signal that the AUB was determined to maintain stability and continue its mission, in spite of all odds. Only those of us who had remained in Lebanon throughout the entire war could fully appreciate the significance of Dr. Waterbury's decision to live on the AUB campus.

Steadily, throughout 1998, conditions in Lebanon and at AUB have been improving. At the hospital, we are no longer troubled by a nursing shortage. Salaries of the staff have been raised and nurses are no longer looking for job opportunities abroad. And for the first time in the history of AUB, we have been able to attract nursing graduates from the University of St. Joseph, a French-oriented institution located in East Beirut. All efforts were made to make them feel welcome at AUB. We wanted this recruitment of French-speaking professionals to work and, thus, encourage others to join us in the future. Thank God all is well. We are now receiving patients from east Beirut, a good indication that the psychological dividing line between East and West Beirut is disappearing.

It was so hard after so many disruptive years to rebuild an atmosphere of credibility and trust among patients, visitors and medical staff. We had to start from scratch. Physically, the hospital was bedraggled and dirty and equipment needed upgrading. The staff, like the children of war, still felt insecure and lacked a clear sense of loyalty and commitment. It will take time, perhaps a new generation,

to regain all we had lost during the war, but with perseverance, I believe we will.

One worrying issue, however, is how people abroad
keep discouraging those coming to work at AUB by paint-
ing a negative image of the country and the hospital. True,
there are disadvantages to life here, but there are also many
aspects of living in Lebanon that can make it a very enrich-
ing experience. I believe those that decide to come should
not come with high expectations; they should not measure
Lebanon with the U.S. in judging the pattern of daily life,
both professionally and socially. If they do that, they will be
disappointed and frustrated. They must accept the country
and its people as they are, enjoy its advantages, and at the
same time make an effort to be instrumental in changing
what needs to be changed. As for the people here, who may
resent the influx of foreigners and fear being replaced by
them, they must put aside their apprehensions and profit
from this transfusion of new energy into the country. The
old-timers must always remember how essential their presence during the war was, and how needed their contributions still are. I have every confidence that with teamwork
and commitment on the part of all, the AUB hospital will
not only regain but also increase its stature as a medical
center of high standards and excellence of care.

As for me, I find myself thirsty for life, eager to make
up for the twenty years of being so engulfed in commitment to a cause. I forgot about myself, my needs, and my
family. I had missed so much—enjoying the pleasures of
young adulthood, having a family of my own, seizing
opportunities to enhance my future. I wonder, again, did
I do right? I only know with certainty that if AUB
needed me again in similar circumstances, I would be
the first to volunteer.

If I feel a sense of loss, it is mostly because I am spending my life so far away from friends and family. To this day, my mother keeps insisting that I return to work and live in America, but this long attachment to AUB, my baby, is still as strong as ever. I have no regrets. For the first time in two decades, my mother and my brothers, George and André, visit me at my home in Lebanon. They finally realize and appreciate my strong commitment to AUB and Lebanon.

As I end my story, I am filled with gratitude toward all those who believed in me and empowered me to make a difference. God bless them, Lebanon, and AUB.

Being decorated by the
Lebanese government
for services rendered,
1975-1995

American University of Beirut

Photo credits:    p. viii    The Moore Collection – American University of Beirut

                  *p. 40      Georges Semerdjian

                  *p. 47      Toufiq Abdallah

                  *p. 67      Sami Ayad

                  *p. 68      An Nahar archives

                  *p. 75      Toufiq Abdallah

                  *p. 80      Georges Semerdjian

                  *p. 82      Ahmed Kywau

                  *p. 87      Sami Ayad

                  *p. 93      Ibrahim Tawil

                  *p. 96      Camille Haddad;

                  *p. 111     Ibrahim Tawil

                  *p. 116     Georges Semerdjian

                  *p. 134     Toufiq Abdallah

                  *p. 136     Toufiq Abdallah

                  *p. 148     Georges Semerdjian

                  *p. 164     Sami Ayad

                  p. 184      The Moore Collection – American University of Beirut

                  *p. 186     Antoine Sarrou';

                  *p. 193     Center Naji Photographique

                  *Purchased from An-Nahar newspaper, Beirut, Lebanon

                  All other photographs were taken by Gladys Mouro